Challenging
Lifestyle

By the same author:
Why Jesus?
Why Christmas?
Questions of Life
Searching Issues
A Life Worth Living
Telling Others
The Heart of Revival
30 Days

See pages 245-248 for more information.

Nicky Gumbel

Challenging Lifestyle

Practical Guidelines for Living Out Jesus' Teachings

Alpha

Alpha Resources
Alpha North America

Challenging Lifestyle
by Nicky Gumbel
Copyright © Nicky Gumbel 1996

4 5 6 7 8 9 10 Printing/Year 04 03 02 01

Published in North America by Alpha Resources, Alpha North America, 74 Trinity Place, New York, NY 10006.

This edition issued by special arrangement with HTB Publications, Brompton Road, London, England SW7 1JA.

Study Guide copyright © by David Stone
Cover and text illustrations by Charlie Mackesy

ISBN 1-931808-163

Contents

Foreword

One of the great challenges for the church today—made harder, I suspect, because the world seems largely to have given up the attempt—is to hold together teaching and ethics.

The Sermon on the Mount is Jesus' teaching on how to conduct our lives. It is His answer to the question, "How exactly can we fulfill our calling to be 'in' the world but not 'of' it?" What could be more important for us in our generation than an earnest attempt to understand and apply this teaching of Jesus?

As we move toward the so-called "post-Christian" era, Nicky Gumbel's choice of material, combined with his experience of life, his humor and his passion for bringing practical sense and sparkle to biblical teaching, has produced an invaluable book for today.

It will prove equally useful to both mature and new Christians, providing excellent follow-up material to the Alpha course, and will help the church to "shine before men, that they may see your good deeds and praise your Father in heaven."

Sandy Millar
Vicar, Holy Trinity Brompton

Preface

With thousands of Alpha courses now running, mainly in the U.K. but now also in many other countries of the world, there is an increasing demand for resources. In particular, there have been many requests for more follow-up material. This book is designed to be part of what will eventually be a two-year program of adult Bible studies. The suggested program now includes the following books: *Questions of Life, A Life Worth Living, Searching Issues* and *Challenging Lifestyle.*

My thanks to those who have so kindly given their time and energy to helping on this project. In particular, I would like to thank Preb. John Collins, the Revd. Paul Perkin, Jo Glen, Helena Hird, Dr. Peter Somers Heslam, Dr. Roland Werner, Patricia Hall, Simon Levell, Chris Russell, Judge Christopher Compston, Helen Adam, Roger Steer, and Andrew Brydon for their helpful comments.

Once again, I am indebted to Jon Soper for his invaluable work as a researcher. Last, but by no means least, my thanks to Philippa Pearson Miles for her extraordinary ability to combine speed and efficiency with charm and good humor.

Nicky Gumbel

Introduction

Now when he saw the crowds, he went up on a mountainside and sat down. His disciples came to him, and he began to teach them.

Our culture is obsessed with lifestyle. There are numerous magazines devoted to clothes, health and fitness, slimming, sexual performance, homes and gardens, and other aspects of lifestyle. They have a preoccupation with style and not content, and are concerned with how things look. Jesus is much more interested in what is underneath.

Jesus' teaching in the Sermon on the Mount presents a challenge to our lifestyle in the West. However, it also offers an alternative: we are called to develop a Christian lifestyle. The question often asked by our culture is not so much "Is Christianity true?" but "Is it real? Does it work?" The world is watching. This is the challenge set before us. As I have preached and worked through the 19 chapters of this book over the last two-and-a-half years, on every occasion I have found myself profoundly challenged by Jesus. I only hope the reader will be as challenged as I have been.

The standards of lifestyle that Jesus sets are very high. The Christian leader John Wimber puts it like this: "Jesus is insatiable. Everything we do pleases Him but nothing satisfies Him. I have been satisfied with Jesus. He has not been satisfied with me. He keeps raising the standards. He walks in high places. He is generous but uncompromising in His call."

11

The Sermon on the Mount has been described as "the supreme jewel in the crown of Jesus' teaching."[1] It is the "Manifesto of the King" and "The Magna Carta of the Kingdom." To say that this is the greatest sermon ever preached would be the understatement of the millennium! As one nineteenth-century commentator put it, "We are near heaven here." [2]

Jesus chose to give this sermon from a mountainside (Matthew 5:1). Perhaps He had in mind that it was on a mountain that Moses received God's commandments in the Old Testament, or it may have been that this was simply the best place to speak.

There is some debate as to whether the sermon is addressed to His disciples or to the crowds. He appears to begin with His disciples (Matthew 5:1) and to finish with everyone listening (Matthew 7:28). The teaching would seem to be primarily for the disciples, the equivalent today of those who are already Christians. But it is clearly appropriate that it be heard by the crowds—comparable, perhaps, to those who are not yet Christians. Jesus continually contrasts the two. He says, "Do not be like them." His disciples should be different both from the non-religious, the Gentiles and pagans (the equivalent today of the secular world), and also from the religious, the scribes and the Pharisees.

Jesus was not laying down a new law to replace the Old Covenant of Moses; He was teaching His followers how to live out the Christian life. Many who are not Christians today claim to live by the teaching of Jesus in the Sermon on the Mount. If they had really read it carefully they would see that it is quite impossible even to begin to live as Jesus taught without the help of His Spirit. Perhaps that was one of the purposes of the sermon. The Reformers in the sixteenth century used to say that the law sends us to Christ to be justified and Christ sends us back to the law to be sanctified. Reading the Sermon on the Mount should make those who do not know Christ and, indeed, all of us, cry out for mercy and help. As we receive Christ and the help of His Spirit, He sends us back to the Sermon on the Mount to learn how to live out our faith. Jesus is teaching us here how to work out what God has worked in.

1
How to Live under God's Blessing

Matthew 5:3–6

> *³Blessed are the poor in spirit,*
>   *for theirs is the kingdom of heaven.*
> *⁴Blessed are those who mourn,*
>   *for they will be comforted.*
> *⁵Blessed are the meek,*
>   *for they will inherit the earth.*
> *⁶Blessed are those who hunger and thirst for righteousness,*
>   *for they will be filled.*

I have never been very good at sports, but I have always enjoyed them. I am a member of a squash club which also has a gym as part of the club. One day I noticed that the gym was running a fitness competition called "The Ultimate Challenge." I love a challenge, so I went to investigate. The competition involved 10 arduous exercises. Each competitor was supposed to train for six weeks beforehand. The circuit could be attempted at different levels: there was "Super Fit," "Fighting Fit," "Getting Fit" and "Older and Wiser." Seeing my emerging gray hairs, it was suggested that I should try "Older and Wiser" or at most "Getting Fit"—especially as I had not done any of the training beforehand. "No," I said, "I would like to do the 'Super Fit' one." This involved, among other things, cycling five kilometers, 40 bench presses at 35 lbs., 50 lap pull-downs at 35 lbs., 100 sit-ups, running one-and-a-half miles uphill at a steep grade, 100 push-ups, and climbing 500 feet on a climbing machine. The whole circuit had to be completed in 45 minutes. Despite attempts by the gym instructors to dissuade me, I was determined to do it at that level.

As I set off I noticed that quite a crowd had gathered. I don't know how I did it, but somehow, pouring with sweat and totally exhausted, I managed to complete the circuit within the time set. I was awarded a $5 gift certificate and a sweatshirt which said on it "I survived the ultimate challenge." Bursting with pride I returned home to show my wife and children the fruit of my achievement. They seemed suitably impressed.

The next day I was a little stiff, but nothing painful. I felt rather pleased with myself. The following day when I woke up I realized something was not quite right. I could not move. Every muscle in my body seemed to have seized up. I could not even get out of bed. I had to be helped out of bed and downstairs. After a lot of gentle stretching I staggered into work, desperately trying to disguise my stiffness in case anyone should find out what a fool I had been. But the first person who saw me walking asked what on earth was wrong with me and I had to spill the beans. I had survived one version of the so-called "Ultimate Challenge," but just barely.

In the Sermon on the Mount, Jesus sets before us an infinitely more important challenge. It is far harder to complete and it takes far longer, but the joy and satisfaction involved are far greater. Unlike the gym exercises it really is "the ultimate challenge." Nobody has ever laid a greater challenge before the world than Jesus did when He preached this sermon. Jesus tells us at the end of the sermon that the person who takes up the challenge is wise.

The importance of this sermon, of which we have probably only an abbreviated form, is underlined by two phrases in the opening verses. First, Jesus "sat down" (vs. 1). When a rabbi sat down to teach, it was a sign that he wanted to say something of great weight and importance. Secondly, "He opened his mouth" (vs. 2, RSV). The Greek expression conveys a solemnity. Perhaps the modern equivalent might be, "He opened His heart."

Right at the start Jesus teaches us about what matters most in life. So often we judge people by what they do: their jobs, their achievements or even what kind of school they went to. Or we may judge them by what they have: wealth, looks, friends, or possessions. Jesus says here that what matters most in life is not what we have or what we do, but who we are. When I was a student at seminary I was no longer "earning a living." It was not so much the lack of money that I felt, but the lack of self-worth. When I was working as a lawyer I was paid for giving my opinion. At seminary, no one was the least bit interested in my opinion! I remember telling a wise Christian how difficult I found this. He said something simple yet so profound. He told me that my experience was a good thing because what matters in life is not what you do but who you are.

Jesus begins the sermon with what Billy Graham has described as eight beautiful attitudes—the Beatitudes. They are like the fruit of the Spirit, in that they are for all Christians. They are not just for a spiritual elite; they are for all the followers of Christ.

The Greek word for "blessed," which appears nine times in the first 11 verses, conveys the idea of happiness, but it means far more than that. Happiness is a subjective feeling. The word used by Jesus means "blessed by God," or "receiving God's favor." The Amplified Version translates it: "Happy, to be envied, and spiritually prosperous, that is with life, joy and satisfaction . . . regardless of . . . outward conditions." Jesus is telling His disciples how they can live their lives under God's blessing.

In the opening verses of the Sermon on the Mount, Jesus answers the question: What sort of people should we be? He describes in eight steps the kind of character we should have. The first four steps are about our relationship with God and we will look at these in this first chapter. The second four are about our relationships with others and we will come to those in Chapter 2.

17

STEP 1—'BLESSED ARE THE POOR IN SPIRIT' (VS. 3)

There are two Greek words for "poor." One means "lacking wealth" and therefore needing to work. The other, which is used here, means to be in such a desperate state of poverty as to be dependent on others for support.

To be "poor in spirit" does not mean having no spiritual backbone; rather, it is the opposite of spiritual pride. It is the opposite of saying, "I have led a morally good life." The person who says that can only have compared their life with others and not with God's standards. To be "poor in spirit" means to recognize how far short we fall in relation to God's standards; to understand that we are up to our eyes in debt and to throw ourselves on the mercy of God. It means saying, with the tax collector, "God, have mercy on me, a sinner" (Luke 18:13). It is the recognition of a desperate need which leads to crying out, "O God, I am in such a mess. I've got nothing to offer. I haven't begun to pray or to hear You properly. I am spiritually blind, naked, and poor." To those who cry out like that Jesus says, "Theirs is the kingdom of heaven" (vs. 3). The kingdom of heaven flings open its doors to beggars.

When we feel spiritually desperate and a complete failure, that is the moment to take heart.

STEP 2—'BLESSED ARE THOSE WHO MOURN' (VS. 4)

The word for "mourn" means "to be sad" or "to grieve." It is frequently used in the Greek translation of the Hebrew Old Testament for mourning over the dead. It is the word used of Jacob's grief when he believed his son was dead (Genesis 37:34–35). Paradoxically, Jesus appears to be saying, "How happy are the unhappy!"

It is a mistake to think that Christians should never be happy, that we should always go around carrying the world's cares on our shoulders and that there should be no joy and no laughter in church. Equally it is a mistake to think that Christians should never be unhappy. As the writer of Ecclesiastes points out, "There is a time for everything . . . a time to weep and a time to laugh, a time to mourn and a time to dance" (Ecclesiastes 3:1, 4).

It is not wrong to weep and mourn at the loss of those we love, just as Jesus wept at the death of Lazarus. We may also weep over the mess we see in the lives of others. Paul wept over the enemies of the cross of Christ (Philippians 3:18). But these types of mourning are not the ones Jesus is speaking about here. Rather it is a weeping at our poverty of spirit. It means not only recognizing our own desperate spiritual poverty, but also being broken-hearted about it.

There is a godly grief which the Spirit of God brings. We see it often at the point of conversion, with weeping over past sins and tears of repentance. Even as Christians, we still make a mess of our lives and need to weep as Peter did when he realized how much he had let Jesus down (Matthew 26:75).

When the Spirit of God comes upon a man or woman the experience is sometimes accompanied by tears. Sometimes past hurts are being healed. Often someone is mourning over opportunities wasted and a sense of spiritual poverty. There is great precedent for God's children weeping, not simply for themselves, but for the cities they are part of and for the land in which they live. Jesus wept over Jerusalem because its inhabitants were so blind to what was going on in their midst. There is such a thing as godly sorrow for our personal and societal spiritual bankruptcy.

Jesus said that when this happened to people, "They will be comforted" (vs. 4). In this age when the Spirit is poured out "on all people" (Acts 2:17), we see how the Spirit of God, known as the Comforter, comes alongside a person and brings them encouragement. He assures them of forgiveness and cleansing and that "in Christ" they are proclaimed righteous. Often, as we observe the ministry of the Holy Spirit, we see tears turn to joy and even laughter, although our comfort will only be complete in heaven.

STEP 3—'BLESSED ARE THE MEEK' (VS. 5)

The Greek word used for "meek" does not mean "weak, spineless, feeble, lifeless, or dreary." It is not the oily cringing of Dickens' Uriah Heep, who constantly describes himself as "your humble servant." Rather it means "gentle, considerate, and unassuming." It means "broken," not in the sense of destroyed or shattered, but in the sense that a horse is broken when it is tamed: strength under submission.

Moses is described as "very meek, more than all men that were on the face of the earth" (Numbers 12:3, RSV). Moses was hardly a weak and spineless leader! But all the force of his character was held in place by God.

The preacher and writer Dr. Martyn Lloyd-Jones defined meekness as "essentially a true view of oneself, expressing itself in attitude and conduct with respect to others." He goes on further to say:

> The man who is meek is not even sensitive about himself. He is not always watching himself and his own interests. He is not always on the defensive. We all know about this, do we not? Is it not one of the greatest curses in life as a result of the Fall—this sensitivity about self? We spend the whole of our lives watching ourselves. But when a man becomes meek he has finished with all that; he no longer worries about himself and what other people say. To be truly meek means we no longer protect ourselves, because we see there is nothing worth defending. So we are not on the defensive; all that is gone. The man who is truly meek never pities himself, he is never sorry for himself.[3]

He goes on to quote John Bunyan: "He that is down need fear no fall."

When we are in this position Jesus says we will "inherit the earth" (vs. 5). Everything we receive is a gift because we know we don't deserve it. When we reach this state we are in a position to know how to receive what God wants to give, both in this life and the life to come—He will give us everything.

STEP 4—'BLESSED ARE THOSE WHO HUNGER AND THIRST FOR RIGHTEOUSNESS' (VS. 6)

"Hunger" and "thirst" are words that most of us in the West simply do not understand. The person who is really hungry (as opposed to having hunger pangs) or the person who is really thirsty (as opposed to just wanting a glass of water) is so desperate that everything else is excluded from their desires.

William Barclay, who was Professor of Divinity and Biblical Criticism at Glasgow University, describes the thirst a person might experience in Palestine in these terms:

> A man might be on a journey, and in the midst of it the hot wind which brought the sandstorm might begin to blow. There was nothing for him to do but to wrap his head in his burnous (a hooded cloak) and turn his back to the wind, and wait, while the swirling sand filled his nostrils and his throat until he was likely to suffocate, and until he was parched with an imperious thirst. In the conditions of modern western life there is no parallel at all to that.[4]

When we are truly desperate, satisfying that hunger or thirst becomes a consuming passion, a grand desire, and an overwhelming ambition.

Jesus says we are to have this attitude toward righteousness. We should long to live in a right relationship with God, to be seen as righteous by Him and to see His righteousness in the society around us. In the Greek New Testament text the word for righteousness is in the accusative case and not the genitive. If it were in the genitive it would mean "to desire partial righteousness"—a slice of the loaf. As it is in the accusative, it means the whole thing—the whole loaf. It means "to desire to be entirely righteous." We are not to be satisfied with anything less than a righteous life; we cannot accept partial goodness. It is not enough to live a Christian life when we feel like it and do what we like at other times. A righteous life is one that is righteous 24 hours a day. It is an integrated Christian life which is lived out in an ongoing relationship, with God affecting everything we do, say, and think.

The problem with many of us is that we are not that desperate. We don't want to pay the price. We say, "Lord, make me holy, but not completely holy quite yet, if You don't mind."

When we are really desperate Jesus says that God will fill us, and our desire for righteousness will be satisfied. It is not enough to see our own spiritual poverty, to mourn over it, and to allow others to draw attention to it. We must also hunger and thirst to be different and to live a righteous life. Jesus promises that the person who follows each of these steps in their relationship with God will be blessed by Him. They will live under God's blessing.

2
How to Have an Influence on Society

Matthew 5:7–16

[7]Blessed are the merciful,
  for they will be shown mercy.
[8]Blessed are the pure in heart,
  for they will see God.
[9]Blessed are the peacemakers,
  for they will be called sons of God.
[10]Blessed are those who are persecuted because of righteousness,
  for theirs is the kingdom of heaven.
[11]Blessed are you when people insult you, persecute you and falsely say all kinds of evil against you because of me.
[12]Rejoice and be glad, because great is your reward in heaven, for in the same way they persecuted the prophets who were before you.
[13]You are the salt of the earth. But if the salt loses its saltiness, how can it be made salty again? It is no longer good for anything, except to be thrown out and trampled by men.
[14]You are the light of the world. A city on a hill cannot be hidden.
[15] Neither do people light a lamp and put it under a bowl. Instead they put it on its stand, and it gives light to everyone in the house. [16] In the same way, let your light shine before men, that they may see your good deeds and praise your Father in heaven.

U.S. Civil Rights leader Martin Luther King, Jr., once said, "A man has not started living until he can rise above the narrow confines of his own existence to the broader concerns of all humanity."

There is something very wrong with our society. We only have to open our newspapers to see a nation torn apart by strife. There is an increasing level of violence and other criminal activity. We see the breakdown of family life cutting across every background, with all the tragic consequences that follow for parents and children alike. The sanctity of human life is under threat with increasing abortion and the desire to allow "mercy-killing." Traditional bases for morality are no longer accepted. Fiona Gibson, editor of the British magazine *More*, speaks for many when she writes in the *Daily Mail*, "If there is a moral code it is: Whatever is pleasurable. It is OK to do whatever you feel like doing."[5]

There is a moral vacuum at the heart of our nation. The West has rejoiced at the collapse of communism, and yet, as Bishop Lesslie Newbigin has pointed out, "Marxism, with all its disastrous failures, at least kept alive the idea that the individual has some kind of responsibility for society." Capitalism, with all its excesses, has been unable to restrain a society which is on the verge of moral bankruptcy. There is a sense of disillusionment with capitalism for its failure to deliver all that it had promised. Politicians seem powerless to shape our society. This moral vacuum inevitably follows the decline of Christian faith. Once the basis of a moral code has been rejected, sooner or later the code itself is questioned.

Not only is there a vacuum at the heart of our nation, but there is also a vacuum in the hearts of individuals. The spiritual hunger in the hearts of human beings remains largely unsatisfied; hunger for meaning and purpose, the desire for permanence, the search for an answer to the problem of guilt, and the longing for community and belonging. With this comes a fascination, which is rooted in fear and uncertainty about life. So more and more are attracted to the cults and the New Age movement, searching in horoscopes or the occult in an urgent attempt to fill this vacuum. What are we to do? We have a choice. Either we can sit back and say, "Well, I'm all right"—if we are. "I have friends and I have all I need. I enjoy life and I never do anyone any harm." We can live a life satisfying our own selfish desires, in what Martin Luther King, Jr., refers to as "the narrow confines of our own existence." Or we can look to "the broader concerns of humanity."

We tend to think that influence comes from wealth or power (military or political) or position. Jesus tells His disciples how they can be an influence for good in their society. Indeed, He tells a small group of ordinary people that they can have an influence on the entire world. The most powerful influence will be not so much what they have or what they do, but who they are. That is why, as we have seen, He starts by teaching them about the sort of people they ought to be.

Jesus said that the first command was to "love the Lord your God with all your heart and with all your soul and with all your mind," and that the second was to "love your neighbor as yourself" (Matthew 22:37–39). In the first chapter we saw that the first four Beatitudes are about our relationship with God. The next four are about our relationships with others.

STEP 5—'BLESSED ARE THE MERCIFUL' (VS. 7)

To be merciful has two slightly different connotations. First, we are to be merciful to those who are in need, like the victim in the parable of the Good Samaritan. We are to look out for those who are hungry, sick, outcast, unpopular, or lonely, and we are to have mercy on them—our mercy will lead naturally to practical help.

Secondly, we are to be merciful to those who have wronged us, even where justice cries out for punishment. This is the opposite to what we see happening all around us in the world, where "tit for tat" and revenge are the order of the day.

Mercy is a divine quality. It is a characteristic of God Himself. Portia described the quality in Shakespeare's *The Merchant of Venice:*

> The quality of mercy is not strain'd,
> It droppeth as the gentle rain from heaven
> Upon the place beneath: it is twice bless'd;
> It blesseth him that gives and him that takes:
> 'Tis mightiest in the mightiest; it becomes
> The throned monarch better than his crown . . .
> It is an attribute to God himself.[6]

Jesus stressed time and again, as He does here, that it is those who show mercy who will receive mercy. It is not that we can earn God's mercy. Rather, the fact that we forgive is evidence that we have been forgiven by God (Luke 7:47). It is not a bargain with God, but a virtuous circle. When we see how much God has forgiven us we cannot fail to have mercy on others (Matthew 18:23–35).

Those who fall into the category of the first four Beatitudes realize how much they need God's mercy. This is the opposite attitude to that of the fault-finder, who is constantly looking for and dwelling on the faults of others. As we have mercy on others we will become increasingly aware of the mercy of God.

John Wimber describes how he was driving home after seeing for the first time a remarkable healing. He was jolted by a vision of a cloud bank superimposed on the sky.

> But I had never seen a cloud bank like this one, so I pulled my car over to the side of the road to take a closer look. Then I realized it was not a cloud bank, it was a honeycomb with honey dripping out onto people below. The people were in a variety of postures. Some were reverent; they were weeping and holding their hands out to catch the honey and taste it, even inviting others to take some of their honey. Others acted irritated, wiping the honey off themselves, complaining about the mess. I was awestruck; not knowing what to think I prayed, "Lord, what is it?" He said, "It's my mercy, John. For some people it's a blessing, but for others it's a hindrance. There's plenty for everyone. . . ." That was a moving and profound experience; certainly it revolutionized my life more than any other experience I had had since becoming a Christian.[7]

STEP 6—'BLESSED ARE THE PURE IN HEART' (VS. 8)

Jesus used to make the point that God is concerned about our hearts, our inward motivation. That is the place where God looks. He is concerned for the inward and moral rather than the outward and ceremonial (Mark 7:1–23). He wants us to have "pure" hearts. The word for "pure" means "unmixed, unadulterated, unalloyed," like pure, clean water.

In a world where the pressure to conform is very great, it means to be free from masks and free from having different roles for different occasions. It means being ourselves as God intended, instead of play-acting; living life in the open and letting people see right through us. The pure in heart are those who are completely sincere in their relationships. They are those who are totally open and have nothing to hide.

Jesus promises that God will reveal Himself to people like that and one day they will see God face to face. Deception blinds us, but purity opens our eyes to see God. The merciful hold nothing against their brothers and sisters. The pure in heart allow others to see them as they are.

STEP 7—'BLESSED ARE THE PEACEMAKERS' (VS. 9)

A peacemaker desires to bring blessing to other people. So many around us lack inner peace. H. G. Wells wrote of Mister Polly, "He was not so much a human being as a civil war."[8] We reflect our inner conflict between each other and realize that it is a small illustration of our lack of peace with God. Hence, this is a call for peace at all three levels: inner peace, peace between people and, most important of all, peace with God.

Jesus says that if we do so we will "be called sons of God" (vs. 9). We will bear the family likeness of our heavenly Father because He is the ultimate peacemaker. Through the cross He made it possible for us to have peace with God (Romans 5:1). The cross has broken down

28

the dividing wall of hostility between people (Ephesians 2:14) and it has made it possible for men and women to be at peace with themselves. This was not peace at any price, but a costly peace; the price was "his one and only Son" (John 3:16).

We are called to reconcile people to God in our evangelism. We implore others to "be reconciled to God" (2 Corinthians 5:20). We know that this is the only route to inner peace which is neither superficial nor deceptive, because it is a peace based on the objective reality of peace with God.

We are called also to bring peace between human beings. That is quite different from doing anything for a peaceful life. Sometimes we need to face up to difficult situations. We may even need to confront in order to make peace. But this is our calling as children of God. This may involve bringing people from apparently irreconcilable positions to a meeting of minds and hearts.

David Armstrong is an Irish Protestant, a Presbyterian, who worked in Magilligan Prison in Northern Ireland. His longing was to see men and women reconciled to God and reconciled to each other. Magilligan Prison used to hold terrorist prisoners for the last years of their sentences. The para-military organizations such as the IRA and the Protestant UVF operated in the jail also. As David prayed and preached about Jesus, many were converted. Jimmy Gibson, a Protestant, was a professional terrorist and had been involved in stirring up other prisoners. As he heard about Jesus he became more and more interested. One day he stopped David in the crowd and said, "I became a Christian last night."

Liam McCloskey was a Roman Catholic and a prominent member of the IRA. He was one of the two original hunger strikers at the Maze prison, part of the dirty protest with Bobby Sands. He would have died had his mother not signed a form giving permission for him to be force-fed. Now this man came to David and said he had just become a Christian by reading his Bible in his cell and wanted to

29

give up his involvement with the IRA. He developed a real concern for the Protestants whom he had previously hated. After their release, Liam McCloskey and Jimmy Gibson traveled together, proclaiming reconciliation through the love of Jesus.[9]

STEP 8—'BLESSED ARE THOSE WHO ARE PERSECUTED BECAUSE OF RIGHTEOUSNESS' (VS. 10)

We might well think that if we live the kind of life that Jesus advocated we would be universally popular. In fact this is not the case. Jesus never guaranteed popularity. In fact, He warns us to be on our guard if everyone thinks highly of us and says that there is bound to be opposition. He never said, "Come to me and your troubles will be over." We are the conscience of mankind and that can be very unpopular. We may have to endure insults and ridicule or even worse.

The early church had a very different attitude from ours in the West when it came to being willing to pay the price of being followers of Jesus Christ. On occasion they found that there was a conflict between their business interest and their loyalty to Jesus Christ. A man once came to the theologian Tertullian (who died around 220 A.D.) with just such a problem. He told him of his business difficulties and ended by saying, "What can I do? I must live!" "Must you?" asked Tertullian.

Jesus never told us to seek persecution, but He did say that when it comes, we are to regard it as a blessing. We are "to rejoice and be glad" (vs. 12) or, as one translation says, "leap for joy." Jesus gives three reasons for doing so. First, because of our reward in heaven. Those who are persecuted because of righteousness are "blessed" because "theirs is the kingdom of heaven" (vs. 10), and in a similar vein He says to His disciples, "Great is your reward in heaven" (vs. 12). Secondly, our joy comes from identifying with Jesus. It is "because of me" (vs. 11) that they are persecuted. Thirdly, it is a sign that our faith is genuine, since the prophets were persecuted in the same way (vs. 12).

The eight attitudes Jesus urges on His disciples are a coherent whole. Matthew uses the literary device of an "inclusio" to show this. Both the first and last Beatitude end with, "For theirs is the kingdom of heaven." These are the attitudes of kingdom citizens. The eight steps can be summarized as follows:

1. Crying out, "O God, have mercy!"
2. Weeping over our condition.
3. Being so broken as to be willing to accept any criticism.
4. Being not only desperate about the past, but longing to do something about the future.
5. Knowing our own need and being merciful to others.
6. Complete openness.
7. Blessing others in every possible way.
8. Expecting nothing in return, except persecution.

Jesus tells this small group of ordinary people that if they live like that they will have an enormous influence on the world around them. And that is what they did.

We are "the salt of the earth" (vs. 13). In days before deep freezers

31

and fridges, salt was used to keep meat from going bad. Christians are called to keep society from decay. More positively, we are called to be "the light of the world" (vs. 14) and to light up the darkness around us.

Jesus, of course, is our model. He described himself as "the light of the world" (John 8:12) and here tells His disciples that they are "the light of the world." Jesus was the most influential person who has ever lived. The historian K. S. Latourette wrote, "Measured by His effect on history, Jesus' is the most influential life ever lived on this planet."[10] One anonymous author described His life in the following way:

> Here is a man who was born in an obscure village, the child of a peasant woman. He grew up in another village. He worked in a carpenter shop until He was 30, and then for three years He was an itinerant preacher. He never owned a home. He never wrote a book. He never held an office. He never had a family. He never went to college. He never put His foot inside a big city. He never traveled 200 miles from the place where He was born. He never did one of the things that usually accompany greatness. He had no credentials but Himself. . . . While still a young man, the tide of popular opinion turned against Him. His friends ran away, one of them denied Him. He was turned over to His enemies. He went through the mockery of a trial. He was nailed upon a cross between two thieves. While He was dying His executioners gambled for the only piece of property He had on earth—His coat. When He was dead, He was taken down and laid in a borrowed grave through the pity of a friend.
>
> Nineteen long centuries have come and gone, and today He is the centerpiece of the human race and the leader of the column of progress. I am far within the mark when I say that all the armies that ever marched, all the navies that ever were built, all the parliaments that ever sat and all the kings that ever reigned, put together, have not affected the life of man upon this earth as powerfully as has that one solitary life.

In order to have an influence on society it is vital, first of all, for Christians not to withdraw from the world into a Christian sub-culture but to get involved in our society. God sent Jesus to get involved in society. He could have remained aloof and safe in heaven, but He chose to get His hands dirty and become immersed in our world. Being "the salt of the earth" (vs. 13), we have "no business to remain snugly in elegant little ecclesiastical salt cellars."[11] Since we are called to be "the light of the world" (vs. 14), we must not put the light in a valley where it cannot be seen, but on a hill (vs. 14). We do not put lamps under bowls but on stands, so that they can give light to the whole house (vs. 15).

So, Jesus says, we must be out there in society letting our lights shine before others so that they may see our good deeds and give praise to God (vs. 16).

As John Stott points out, "Christians have been blaming the meat (of society) for going rotten when the preserving salt has been taken out of it, and the house for getting darker when the light has been removed. It is time for Christians to recognize their responsibility to be salt and light in our society."[12] Or as someone else has put it, "If the world is in the soup, that is where the salt needs to be."

Christians need to be salt and light in their work environments.

That is why we should not give up working in a secular environment unless we are specifically called out of it. We are called to have an influence in the office, factory, police force, hospital, shop, or wherever it is that we are working. This is where frontline ministry takes place.

We are called also to be salt and light in our neighborhoods and in our leisure activities. Sports, for example, offer ideal opportunities to get involved in local teams and clubs and to pray that we may be able to influence people there for Christ.

Further, we are called to play our part as citizens. For some this means direct involvement in local or national politics. All of us are called to speak out on issues that conflict with Christianity; to fight for justice, freedom, dignity of the individual, and the abolition of discrimination as well as taking social action to help those who are casualties of our society.

Nor does this calling end at our own shores. We live in a world with massive needs. Millions have yet to hear the good news about Jesus Christ. Two-thirds of the world's population suffer chronic food deficiencies. Injustice abounds in every society as human rights are continually violated and the poor are constantly oppressed. John Stott observes that for many, the greatest threat to the human race is the threat of irreversible damage to the environment. The Bible teaches that both God and men have rights in and responsibilities toward the earth, rather like a landlord and tenant. Mismanagement on our part is a sin against God as well as humankind. Christians should be responsible, ecological stewards.[13]

While it is easy to feel daunted and overwhelmed by the scale of these problems, there is much we can do. Some will be called to devote their whole lives to the alleviation of global suffering and may, like Mother Teresa or Jackie Pullinger, have an influence far beyond their expectations. All of us can be aware of the problems, advocate the cause of the poor, and support with our prayers and our money those agencies which are working so effectively in the sphere of Christian service.

Secondly, while not withdrawing from the secular world, if we are to be effective in our Christian influence we must remain distinctive from it. The salt is different from the meat. The light is different from the world. Jesus warned that "if the salt loses its saltiness, how can it be made salty again? It is no longer good for anything, except to be thrown out and trampled by men" (Matthew 5:13). We are called to live a radically different lifestyle from that of the world around us. If we have the character that Jesus describes in the Beatitudes, there is no doubt that we will be radically different. It could be summarized as loving God with all our hearts and loving our neighbors as ourselves. Others will see humility, openness, truthfulness, hard work, reliability, the avoidance of gossip, the desire to build up and encourage others, unselfishness, kindness, and all the fruit of the Spirit (Galatians 5:22–23).

Thirdly, if we are to have an influence we must let our light shine before others, "that they may see your good deeds and praise your Father in heaven" (vs. 16). Once again Jesus is our example. His praying, fasting, and giving were private (as He taught His disciples to do), but His good works were public. He proclaimed the Gospel, healed the sick, raised the dead, set the captives free, and fed the hungry. It is because the disciples followed His example that they had such an enormous influence on society. K. S. Latourette sums it up at the conclusion of his seven-volume *History of the Expansion of Christianity*. He refers in glowing terms to the effects of the life of Christ through his followers:

> No life ever lived on this planet has been so influential in the affairs of men. . . . From that brief life and its apparent frustration has flowed a more powerful force for the triumphal waging of man's long battle than any other ever known by the human race. . . . Through it hundreds of millions have been lifted from illiteracy and ignorance, and have been

placed upon the road of growing intellectual freedom and of control over their physical environment. It has done more to allay the physical ills of disease and famine than any other impulse known to man. It has emancipated millions from chattel slavery and millions of others from thraldom to vice. It has protected tens of millions from exploitation by their fellows. It has been the most fruitful source of movements to lessen the horrors of war and to put the relations of men and nations on the basis of justice and peace.[14]

I began this chapter with a quote from Martin Luther King, Jr. I want to end with an excerpt from the sermon he preached at Ebenezer Baptist Church on February 4, 1968, two months before he was assassinated, and which was played at his funeral.

Every now and then I guess we all think realistically about that day when we will be victimized with what is life's final common denominator—that something we call death. We all think about it. And every now and then I think about my own death, and I think about my own funeral. And I don't think of it in a morbid sense. Every now and then I ask myself, "What is it that I would want said?" And I leave the word to you this morning.

If any of you are around when I have to meet my day, I don't want a long funeral. And if you get somebody to deliver the eulogy, tell them not to talk too long. Every now and then I wonder what I want them to say. Tell them not to mention that I have a Nobel Peace Prize, that isn't important. Tell them not to mention that I have three or four hundred other awards, that's not important. Tell them not to mention where I went to school.

I'd like somebody to mention that day that Martin Luther King tried to give his life serving others. I'd like for somebody to say that day that Martin Luther King tried to love somebody. I want you to say that day that I tried to be right on the war question. I want you to be able to say that day that I did try to feed the hungry. And I want you to be able to say that day that I did try, in my life, to clothe those who were naked. I want you to say on that day that I did try, in my life, to visit those who were in prison. I want you to say that I tried to love and serve humanity. Yes, if you want to say that I was a drum major, say that I was a drum major for justice. Say that I was a drum major for peace, I was a drum major for righteousness. And all of the other shallow things will not matter. I won't have any money to leave behind. I won't have the fine and luxurious things of life to leave behind. I just want to leave a committed life behind.

And that's all I want to say . . . if I can help somebody as I pass along, if I can cheer somebody with a word or song, if I can show somebody he's traveling wrong, then my living will not be in vain.

If I can do my duty as a Christian ought, if I can bring salvation to a world over wrought, if I can spread the message as the Master taught, then my living will not be in vain.[15]

3
How to Understand the Old Testament
Matthew 5:17–20

¹⁷Do not think that I have come to abolish the Law or the Prophets; I have not come to abolish them but to fulfill them. ¹⁸I tell you the truth, until heaven and earth disappear, not the smallest letter, not the least stroke of a pen, will by any means disappear from the Law until everything is accomplished. ¹⁹Anyone who breaks one of the least of these commandments and teaches others to do the same will be called least in the kingdom of heaven, but whoever practices and teaches these commands will be called great in the kingdom of heaven. ²⁰For I tell you that unless your righteousness surpasses that of the Pharisees and the teachers of the law, you will certainly not enter the kingdom of heaven.

In the second century A.D., Marcion was a wealthy shipowner and the son of a bishop. He was a superb organizer and built up communities over a large part of the Roman Empire. His central thesis was that the Christian gospel is wholly a gospel of love to the absolute exclusion of law. He rejected the Old Testament in its entirety. This rejection of the Old Testament led him to cut out much of the New Testament as well. He rejected all the writings of the apostles except Paul, who was his hero. He accepted 10 of his letters after making some alterations. With the gospels he was more cavalier. He rejected all but Luke and since Luke showed every sign of acknowledging the validity of the Old Testament, considerable parts of this book had to go as well. He demonstrated the principle that if you take the scissors to the Bible it is very difficult to know where to stop cutting. In 144 A.D. he was excommunicated for immorality.

Most ancient heresies have their modern equivalents. Many today are very selective and want to serve God only in an advisory capacity. They say that they like the teaching of Jesus but do not like the God of the Old Testament. Others, while formally accepting the Old Testament as part of God's revelation in practice, do not consider it of great importance and never read it. They agree with the small boy who referred to the Old Testament as the time "before God became a Christian"! There are also those who, like Marcion, see the gospel of love taught by Jesus as contradicting and abolishing the law.

In this chapter I want to look at Jesus' attitude to the Old Testament and what our attitude should be in the light of His.[16]

Obviously Jesus never read the New Testament! To Him the Scriptures were the Old Testament. Jesus stamped the entire Old Testament with His seal of authority (vss. 17–18). The Old Testament is sometimes referred to as "the Law and the Prophets" (vs. 17) and sometimes as simply "the Law" (vs. 18). (Elsewhere, it is referred to as "the law, the prophets and the writing.") Jesus said that He was not abolishing the Old Testament. Rather He was endorsing every word of it. He said, "Not the smallest letter, not the least stroke of a pen, will by any means disappear from the Law until everything is accomplished" (vs. 18). Jesus taught that "the Scripture cannot be broken" (John 10:35). What the Scripture said, God said (Matthew 19:4–5). He read it, quoted it, believed it, and lived by it. Theologian John Wenham sums up Jesus' view of the Old Testament: "To Christ, the Old Testament was true, authoritative, inspired. To Him, the God of the Old Testament was the living God, and the teaching of the Old Testament was the teaching of the living God. To Him, what Scripture said, God said."[17]

When Jesus said He did not come to abolish the Old Testament but to fulfill it, what did He mean?

The Old Testament is a library of 39 books. There are three main ways to look at the Old Testament. One way to look at it is as the acts of God in *history*. History is "His story." The Old Testament is an account of salvation-history. In the Old Testament we see the history of God's relationship with human beings from Creation, the Fall, and the Flood. We see the people of God from Abraham and Joseph, from the Exodus to the wilderness and the Conquest. We read of the Judges and the monarchy, the Exile and the return from Exile. How are we to understand all this? What relevance does it have to our lives today?

Another way of looking at the Old Testament is in terms of *promise*. The Old Testament is full of hope and expectation. We read of the promises to Noah, Abraham, Moses, and David. Then, in the Prophets, we see how God spoke to the people of Israel. The former Prophets are the books of Joshua, Judges, 1 and 2 Samuel and 1 and 2 Kings. They describe the early history of Israel. The latter prophets include Isaiah, Jeremiah, Ezekiel, and Daniel, and 12 other less-known characters: Hosea, Joel, Amos, Obadiah, Jonah, Micah, Nahum, Habakkuk, Zephaniah, Haggai, Zechariah, and Malachi.

A third way of looking at the Old Testament is in terms of *law*. Some scholars have found it helpful to see the first five books of the

Bible as moral law, civil law, and ceremonial law. The Hebrew word for law, *torah*, really means "guidance" or "instruction."

Jesus said that He did not come to abolish the Old Testament but to fulfill it. The theme of fulfillment runs through the New Testament and it is especially drawn out in Matthew's Gospel. Matthew shows how Jesus fulfilled each of these three views of the Old Testament and in turn shows us how to understand the Old Testament.

JESUS FULFILLS SALVATION-HISTORY

Matthew begins his Gospel, not with the birth of Jesus, but by summarizing the Old Testament story in terms of Jesus' ancestry (Matthew 1:1–17). For Matthew the Old Testament tells the story that Jesus completes. He sets out the history of the people of God in terms of three equal periods: the 14 generations from Abraham to David, 14 generations from David to the Exile, and 14 from the Exile to Christ (vs. 17). In the genealogy, biological generations are skipped over (as was quite common in Old Testament genealogy). He is pointing out that Old Testament history falls into three approximately equal spans of time between crucial events. Jesus is the end of the line as far as the Old Testament story goes—the climax has been reached.

This is the story from which Jesus acquired His identity and mission. It is also the story to which He gave significance and authority. As we read the Old Testament it makes a difference to know that it leads to Jesus and He gives meaning to it. How then are we to understand the Old Testament in the light of the fact that Jesus completes the story?

First, the reality of the Old Testament story is affirmed. The Old Testament is more than just prediction about Jesus. It is the story of the acts of God in human history out of which promises arise and in relation to which they make sense. The stories tell us about a true, real relationship between God and His people and a real revelation of God to His people. For example, the story of the Exodus tells us about His care for the oppressed, the poor, and the suffering. It tells of His action for justice on behalf of the exploited. It tells us of a God of redemption who sets His people free.

Secondly, Jesus sheds light backward on the story. We understand a story in the light of its destination. The Old Testament cannot be fully understood without Jesus. Jesus once said to the Pharisees, who knew their Old Testaments in the utmost detail, "You diligently study the Scriptures because you think that by them you possess eternal life. These are the Scriptures that testify about me, yet you refuse to come to me to have life" (John 5:39–40). If we go into a dark room full of furniture, we may be able to make out something of what is there by feeling the sofas, chairs, and pictures. When the light is switched on we are able to see the whole room in a completely different way. So with the light of Jesus we are able to see the whole Old Testament with an additional level of significance. As Augustine of Hippo put it, "The new is in the old concealed. The old is in the new revealed."

Thirdly, the Old Testament story helps us gain a full understanding of Christ. Just as it is possible to watch the last act of a play and get a great deal out of it, so it is possible to read the New Testament on its own. However, it helps to watch the earlier acts of the play as well if we are going to understand the climax and conclusion. In order to understand Jesus we need to read the earlier acts of God in our salvation-history.

JESUS FULFILLS GOD'S PROMISE

As we have seen, another way to look at the Old Testament is in terms of promise. In the Bible, the Old Testament ends with prophecy, because the early Christians saw the Old Testament as a promise which Jesus fulfilled. We have also seen that Matthew starts his Gospel with Jesus completing the Old Testament story (Matthew 1:1–17). Then he moves on to Jesus fulfilling Old Testament prophecy. He ties up each of five scenes from the conception, birth, and early childhood of Jesus to the Hebrew Scriptures which have been "fulfilled" by the events described (Matthew 1:22; 2:5–6, 17, 23; 4:14–16). Jesus is not only the completion of the Old Testament story at a historical level, He is also the fulfillment of the Old Testament at the level of promise.

If we look at the Old Testament prophecies in terms of prediction we can see how many Jesus fulfilled. His birth in Bethlehem, His early life in Nazareth, His miracles of healing, His betrayal, His suffering, His death between thieves, His burial, resurrection, ascension, and the outpouring of the Spirit were all predicted in the Old Testament and fulfilled by Jesus in the New Testament. He fulfilled over 300 prophecies, including 29 in a single day, spoken by different voices over a 500-year period. After His resurrection, on the road to Emmaus, Jesus took the two disciples through the Old Testament: "Beginning with Moses and all the Prophets, he explained to them what was said in all the Scriptures concerning himself" (Luke 24:27).

However, when we say that Jesus fulfilled the promises of the Old Testament we mean more than that He did what had been predicted. The Old Testament is not just a series of predictions. The word "testament" means "covenant." At the heart of the word "covenant" is the idea of promise. The Old Testament is about the promises of God given on His initiative, requiring a human response. This can be seen in all the Old Testament covenants, with Noah, Abraham, Moses and the people of Israel, and with David. We see the rich array of the promises of God, like different streams leading to a great river. In the end they all combine into a single current, flowing deep and strong, the ongoing irresistible promise of God finding its climax in a new covenant with the life, death, and Resurrection of Jesus of Nazareth.

The promises were made in terms already within the experience and comprehension of those who received them. The Old Testament promises are not always fulfilled in the literal form originally given. The fulfillment in terms of what God did in Christ is at a different level of reality. Suppose in 1950 a man promised his young son a black and white TV set on his twenty-first birthday. When the time came he gave him a color TV which had not existed at the time the promise was made. Would the son complain that the promise had not been fulfilled? Would he go on looking for a literal fulfillment? No, because the reality far surpasses the original promise.

JESUS FULFILLS GOD'S LAW

The third way to look at the Old Testament is in terms of law. Indeed, we have seen that Jesus Himself refers to the Old Testament as "the law" (vs. 18). In his prologue Matthew shows that Jesus fulfills the Old Testament story (Matthew 1:1–17), and in the next section He shows that Jesus fulfills the Old Testament promise (Matthew 1:18–4:16). In the Sermon on the Mount he shows that Jesus fulfills the Old Testament by revealing the full depth and meaning of the Old Testament law.

The law was given as part of God's blessing to His people, in the context of the covenant (Exodus 20). The law was intended for their good, to protect them from harm, and to bring them prosperity and life (Deuteronomy 6:24). It was not a means of salvation, but a response to salvation. The motive for keeping the law was gratitude for what God had done for them in bringing them out of Egypt (Exodus 20:2). In keeping the law they would be imitating God (Leviticus 19:2).

It is a mistake to think that the Old Testament itself is legalistic or that Jesus repudiated the Old Testament law.[18] What He attacked in the Sermon on the Mount was the scribal misinterpretations of the law. The scribes and Pharisees had found 248 commands and 365 prohibitions in the Old Testament. In the Mishnah and the Talmud,

44

which embody Jewish oral law, they added their own interpretation of these laws, in order to put a hedge of protection around the law and to avoid any possible transgression.

Jesus says in these verses that He has not come to abolish the Old Testament law; rather, He has come to fill it out and to reveal the full depth of its meaning. What He goes on to show in the rest of the sermon is that this meaning is not outward and concerned with external observance, but inward and moral. He interprets it not by adding new rules, but by showing that at the heart of the law is the law of the heart, the law of mind and motive. He shows what the law really means in terms of anger, lust, fidelity, integrity, and care for others. He called His disciples to a righteousness that surpassed that of the scribes and Pharisees (vs. 20). He was not contradicting the Old Testament, but going in the same direction. He was building on it and surpassing it, whereas the scribal misinterpretations were going in the opposite direction in that they led to legalism.

Jesus summarized the law as loving God and loving our neighbor (Matthew 22:37–40). We need this summary to keep us from legalism. On the other hand we need the detailed breakdown of the laws to keep us from sentimentality. It is no good thinking that adultery is "loving our neighbor" when adultery is specifically forbidden. The laws of the road could be summarized as, "Drive carefully and considerately." That is what really matters. On the other hand we need the detailed rules to tell us how to drive carefully and considerately.

So Jesus fulfilled the Old Testament law by showing us what it really meant. He also fulfilled the law in the sense that He lived it out. He is the only person who has ever done this because only He has ever lived a sinless life. As German theologian Dietrich Bonhoeffer said about Jesus and the Old Testament laws, "He has in fact nothing to add except this, that He keeps them."[19] He lived a righteous life. His righteousness far exceeded that of the scribes and the Pharisees. He showed us how to live a righteous life.

But He did not leave us there. He also fulfilled the law in that He made it possible for us to live a righteous life. Through His death and resurrection, He set us free from the power of sin and provided for us a righteousness that comes from God (Romans 3:21–26). He enabled the Spirit of God to be poured out.

> What the law was powerless to do in that it was weakened by the sinful nature, God did by sending his own Son in the likeness of sinful man to be a sin offering. And so he condemned sin in sinful man, in order that the righteous requirements of the law might be fully met in us, who do not live according to the sinful nature but according to the Spirit (Romans 8:3–4).

Marcion was wrong. To reject the Old Testament is to reject the clear teaching of Jesus. Jesus did not reject it. He endorsed and fulfilled it. The gospel of love is not opposed to the Old Testament; rather it is complementary. The Gospel sets us free from the condemnation of the law (Romans 8:1–2), but not from the commands. Rather Jesus gives us the desire and the power to fulfill the real meaning of the law and to live righteous lives.

To summarize:

> The Old Testament tells the story which Jesus completed. It declares the promise which He fulfilled. It provides the pictures and models which shaped His identity. It programs a mission which He accepted and passed on. It teaches the moral orientation to God and the world which He endorsed, sharpened, and laid as the foundation for obedient discipleship.[20]

We need to be reading the Old Testament regularly, seeking to understand it not only in terms of the culture and history in which it was written, but also, ultimately, in the light of Jesus' fulfillment of it.

Then we need to go back to the New Testament and reread that with a fresh understanding of who Jesus was and is.

4
How to Deal with Anger

Matthew 5:21–26

²¹ You have heard that it was said to the people long ago, "Do not murder, and anyone who murders will be subject to judgment." ²² But I tell you that anyone who is angry with his brother will be subject to judgment. Again, anyone who says to his brother, "Raca," is answerable to the Sanhedrin. But anyone who says, "You fool!" will be in danger of the fire of hell.

²³ Therefore, if you are offering your gift at the altar and there remember that your brother has something against you, ²⁴ leave your gift there in front of the altar. First go and be reconciled to your brother; then come and offer your gift.

²⁵ Settle matters quickly with your adversary who is taking you to court. Do it while you are still with him on the way, or he may hand you over to the judge, and the judge may hand you over to the officer, and you may be thrown into prison. ²⁶ I tell you the truth, you will not get out until you have paid the last penny.

A young girl who was writing an essay for school came to her father and asked, "Dad, what is the difference between anger and exasperation?" The father replied, "It is mostly a matter of degree. Let me show you what I mean." With that her father went to the telephone and dialed a number at random. To the man who answered the phone, he said, "Hello, is Melvin there?" The man answered, "There is no one here called Melvin. Why don't you learn to look up numbers before you dial them?" "See," said the father to his daughter. "That man was not a bit happy with our call. He was probably very busy with something and we annoyed him. Now watch. . . ." The father dialed the number again. "Hello, is Melvin there?" asked the

47

father. "Now look here!" came the heated reply. "You just called this number and I told you that there is no Melvin here! You've got a lot of nerve calling again!" The receiver was slammed down hard. The father turned to his daughter and said, "You see that was anger. Now I'll show you what exasperation means." He again dialed the same number and when a violent voice roared "Hello!" the father calmly said, "Hello, this is Melvin. Have there been any calls for me?"

There is also a serious side to anger. Many today regard anger as part of self-assertion. Gael Lindenfield, a psychotherapist running courses in personal development, suggests that we should write down a list like this and read it through several times:

1. I have a right to feel angry when I am frustrated.
2. I have a right to feel angry when I am disheartened.
3. I have a right to feel angry when I am hurt.
4. I have a right to feel angry when I am attacked.
5. I have a right to feel angry when I am oppressed.
6. I have a right to feel angry when I am exploited.
7. I have a right to feel angry when I am manipulated.
8. I have a right to feel angry when I am cheated.

9.   I have a right to feel angry when my needs are ignored.
10. I have a right to feel angry when I am let down.
11. I have a right to feel angry when I am rejected.[21]

In contrast, Jesus seems to be suggesting in this passage that such an approach to anger is wrong. He makes a contrast, not between the law given through Moses and his teaching, but between a false interpretation of Moses and a true interpretation. Moses said, "You shall not murder" (Exodus 20:13), and the word "murder" indicates a criminal killing. The false interpretation is to limit the command to the physical act of murder. Jesus traces murder back to the secret place of the human heart where the thought processes which lead to murder begin.

What is He saying about anger? Is all anger wrong? Is there such a thing as constructive anger? How should we deal with our anger? These are some of the questions I want to look at in this chapter.

ANGRY FEELINGS (VSS. 21–22)

Jesus says, "But I tell you that anyone who is angry with his brother will be subject to judgment" (vs. 22). Some manuscripts add the words "without cause." These words are not in the earliest texts of Matthew's Gospel, but arguably they are a correct interpretation of Jesus' teaching. Not all anger is wrong. Jesus Himself was angry at times. Matthew, along with the other Gospel writers, recalls how He angrily overturned the tables of the money changers in the temple area (Matthew 21:12). He called the Pharisees "You blind fools!" (Matthew 23:17). On one occasion, when He saw their "stubborn hearts" and a lack of compassion for the sick, Jesus looked at them "in anger" (Mark 3:1–6).

So there is such a thing as righteous anger. In the Old Testament there are 20 different words for "wrath" and between them they are used 580 times. The prophets and the psalmists use the strongly personal terms when they speak of the anger of the Lord (e.g., Isaiah 30:27; Jeremiah 23:20; Ezekiel 8:8). His anger is part of His holy love, a flame that sears and purifies. There is no moral flabbiness in God. Anger is God's personal reaction to sin. The anger of Jesus was directed against sin and injustice; it was the judicial anger as one who was given authority by God to judge. His personal ego was not wrapped up in His anger. When He was arrested, unfairly tried, tortured, and then crucified, "he did not retaliate; when he suffered, he made no threats" (1 Peter 2:23). When hanging in agony, attacked, oppressed, exploited, hurt, and rejected He did not say, "I have a right to feel angry." Rather He said, "Father, forgive. . . ." (Luke 23:34).

For the rest of us too, there is a place for righteous anger. Indignation against wickedness is surely an essential element of human goodness in a world in which moral evil is always present. A person who knows, for example, about the injustice and cruelty of apartheid or the evil of terrorism or the sexual abuse of children and is not angry at such wickedness cannot be a thoroughly good person. Our lack of anger means a failure to care for our fellow human beings, a failure of love.

Anger is a natural passion. Physically, it causes many changes in our bodies. Adrenaline flows, hunger disappears, we have a clearer and more focused vision, an increased supply of the male hormone testosterone, and glucose is freed from the reserves of our livers. All this can be channeled in a constructive way. Martin Luther (1483–1546) wrote, "When I am angry I can write, pray, and preach well, for then my whole temperament is quickened, my understanding sharpened, and all mundane vexations and temptations depart." We need men and women like Luther today, who will be roused with a passion which includes anger, who will see the evil that exists in the Church and the world and will be driven to do something about it.

The difficulty we face as fallen human beings is making sure we do not sin when we are angry. Paul wrote, "In your anger do not sin" (Ephesians 4:26). Over 300 years earlier Aristotle (348–322 B.C.) wrote, "Anybody can become angry—that is easy; but to be angry with the right person and to the right degree and at the right time, and for the right purpose, and in the right way—that is not within everybody's power and is not easy." Our anger tends, on the whole, to be unrighteous. Unlike Jesus, we get angry because we are hurt, jealous, proud, or arrogant, our toes have been stepped on or our noses put out of joint.

Perhaps this is seen most clearly, on occasions, in sport.

A cricketer named Bryn Derbyshire who had been called out, reversed his car at high speed at the umpire, who hurt his arm as he leapt clear. Members of the opposing team came to the rescue and one smashed the sun roof of Derbyshire's car with a cricket bat.

In court Derbyshire, aged 37, admitted causing bodily harm by wanton furious driving after the match between his team, Old Park, of Nottingham, and a side from Blyth, Nottinghamshire. Nottingham Crown Court gave him a three-month suspended sentence and ordered him to pay $750 to the 59-year-old umpire, Joseph Purser.

Afterward Mr. Purser said: "I stand by my decision. He was out." [22]

Much of our anger is selfish rather than loving anger. What Jesus is saying is that we do *not* have a right to feel angry when we are frustrated, disheartened, or hurt, because we lay down this right as Jesus Himself did.

There are two Greek words for anger. The word used here means "long-lived anger," the anger of a person who nurses wrath to keep it warm. It means "anger that broods, refuses to be pacified, and seeks revenge." Jesus says that these angry feelings may not be capable of being examined in a human court, but they are accountable in the court of heaven (vs. 22).

Jesus sees anger as the root of murder. The process starts with angry feelings, then if they are nursed, hatred follows, and if unchecked, the fruit is sometimes actual murder. John makes the same point when he says, "Anyone who hates his brother is a murderer" (1 John 3:15). As Philip Henry (1631–1696) put it: "When anger was in Cain's heart, murder was not far off." Jesus says that the place to begin is early on, with the initial feelings of anger. They need to be dealt with ruthlessly.

ANGRY WORDS (VS. 22)

Jesus goes on to warn that angry words are as bad as or even worse than angry feelings. Again Lindenfield urges us to express our anger. She warns against being "too nice." She suggests that unexpressed anger is positively harmful, causing depression, teenage suicides, riots, and malicious behavior.

It is true that we do need positive outlets for our feelings, but Jesus warns us of the danger of unbridled expressions of anger. He says, "Anyone who says to his brother, 'Raca,' is answerable to the Sanhedrin. But anyone who says, 'You fool!' will be in danger of the fire of hell" (vs. 22). The word "Raca" is an Aramaic term which conveys contempt for a person's mind. It is the equivalent of calling someone a moron, a stupid imbecile, or a brainless idiot. The Greek word for "fool" suggests contempt for their heart or character. It labels them as a moral fool or a scoundrel. Some have tried to suggest that these two words that Jesus used are particularly objectionable words. But that is to misunderstand His message. Jesus is using examples of the lightest terms of abuse and warning us of their danger.

Angry words pierce the heart. They are intended to hit, hurt, and destroy. They are extremely damaging to relationships and if left unchecked they can even lead to murder. Recently, I heard a mother of a small child with whom she was very angry, shouting at the child, "I'll kill you!" Jesus is warning here that such words break the sixth commandment.

Of course, loving confrontation is sometimes necessary and children need discipline. Disagreements need to be brought out into the open. Truth is more important than a superficial peace. Personal growth involves being willing to learn from criticism as well as encouragement. Jesus is not suggesting a suppression of all feelings and emotions. Rather He is warning against reacting out of anger because we have been hurt in some way.

Nor is this a minor matter. The threat of judgment was part of the Mosaic legislation dealing with murder. The murderer would appear before a human court and be judged. Jesus warns that angry feelings and words are equally subject to judgment. Calling a brother "Raca" renders the person liable to the Sanhedrin (the highest Jewish court in the land). Calling him a fool puts him in danger of hell. Gehenna, the name Jesus uses here, was the valley of Hinnem, the ravine south of Jerusalem where rubbish was dumped and burned. Jesus often used the word as a picture of the final judgment. The list of judgments is not an escalating succession of threats, but a warning that God is behind all judgment, based on His assessment of the heart and that feelings and words can lead to ultimate destruction. He is not equating angry words and feelings with murder, but using the language of hyperbole to warn of the dangers of vengeful anger.

When Jesus died on the cross, He set us free from anger, together with all other sins. Sometimes, the change will take place instantaneously. Before we were married, my wife Pippa shared a flat with another young woman who was a nurse and worked very long hours. Whenever this woman overslept she would let out a torrent of angry words as she woke up in anger and frustration. After they had been sharing the house for a year, this woman gave her life to Christ. The following morning she overslept again. Pippa woke her up and was amazed to find that there was no torrent of angry words. An extraordinary change had occurred in her life.

DEALING WITH ANGER (VSS. 23–26)

The teaching of Jesus in this area is very positive. First, when there is a Christian with whom we are very angry, Jesus says that we are to *settle out of church*. Disharmony destroys the church. When Christians get angry with one another, when they attack and insult their brothers and sisters, the Body of Christ is split.

Secondly, Jesus says we are to *settle out of court*. He takes us from the Temple to the courtroom, or rather just outside the courtroom, and says:

> Settle matters quickly with your adversary who is taking you to court. Do it while you are still with him on the way, or he may hand you over to the judge, and the judge may hand you over to the officer, and you may be thrown into prison. I tell you the truth, you will not get out until you have paid the last penny (vss. 25–26).

Under Roman law there were certain crimes such as theft, burglary, and kidnapping, for which the offender could be subject to summary arrest. If the criminal was caught red-handed, the offended citizen caught hold of the man's robe at the throat and held him in a stranglehold so that he could not escape. If the defendant was found guilty, he was handed over to the court officer whose duty it was to ensure that the penalty was paid. He had the power to imprison defaulters, who would not get out until they had paid the last "penny." The Greek word refers to an infinitesimal sum.

This is not an allegory, so we cannot apply every detail. Rather it is a parable, in which Jesus warns us of the dangers of getting involved in quarrels and especially in litigation. The nineteenth-century preacher, C. H. Spurgeon, commenting on these verses, pointed out that "a lean settlement is better than a fat lawsuit," and remarked, "Many go into the court to get wool, but come out closely shorn." [23] I know from my own experience practicing as an attorney how true this is. I have seen many cases in which both parties would

have been far better off if only they could have settled these differences without the need of a court case. Often it is unresolved anger
which spurs the parties on, in spite of the consequences.

Jesus urges us to "settle matters quickly" (vs. 25). In many ways,
anger is like dry rot. When we moved into our house, we discovered
a small portion of rot on a door frame. As we began to look for the
source, we discovered that the whole basement was riddled with dry
rot. Apparently, in the right conditions it can spread up to three feet
in a week. For the most part it is hidden behind walls and door
frames, and in the beginning it is hard to see. If left unchecked it
brings sudden devastation. The only way to deal with it is quickly and
with drastic action.

In the same way, we need to deal immediately with anger in
relationships and take drastic action. Unless we do so, it will destroy
marriages, relationships, churches, and organizations.

The way to deal with anger is to engage in reconciliation. We are
to take positive steps to restore relationships. Jesus says, "Therefore,
if you are offering your gift at the altar and there remember that
your brother has something against you, leave your gift there in front
of the altar. First go and be reconciled to your brother; then come
and offer your gift" (vss. 23–24).

The lay worshiper brought his gift, along with an animal or
otherwise, to the temple for sacrifice. It is implied that he has been
in the wrong. Jesus says there is no point in offering the gift until he
is reconciled with his brother. Jesus points out that our anger in
human relationships erects a barrier, not only between us and other
brothers and sisters in Christ, but also between us and God.

It is not just our own anger which creates this barrier. If we are
conscious that we have angered someone else we must equally cease
worship and seek reconciliation. Ugandan Bishop Festo Kivengere
told how he was going off to preach after a row with his wife. The
Holy Spirit said to him, "Go back and pray with your wife!"

He argued, "I'm due to preach in 20 minutes. I'll do it afterward."

"OK," said the Holy Spirit. "You go and preach; I'll stay with your wife." [24]

Worship cannot be detached from conduct. They are inextricably linked. In one sense, our conduct flows from our worship. In another sense, it is only when our conduct is right that we are in a right mind to worship God. This is what the prophets pointed out over and over again (Isaiah 1:10–17; Jeremiah 7:9–11; Amos 5:21–24; Micah 6:6–8).

CONCLUSION

The standard Jesus sets in this passage is extraordinarily high. It is His first example of an area in which we are called to a "righteousness [which] surpasses that of the Pharisees and the teachers of the law" (vs. 20). We all fall so far short of His standards. In a sermon on this passage, Bill Hybels, pastor of Willow Creek church in Illinois, spoke of his nightmare that one day he will be standing before the throne of judgment and will find himself in a line behind Mother Teresa and hear God say to her, "You really fell a long way short of my ideals!"

As we read this passage, surely we are all conscious of our own failings and weaknesses. We are brought back to the cross to cry out for mercy and forgiveness. The forgiveness we received gives us the strength to forgive and seek reconciliation. As we see what our offenses did to Jesus, we cannot be angry any longer with our brothers and sisters.

Dealing with anger involves both receiving and giving forgiveness, through the cross of Christ. It requires a determined act of the will to deal ruthlessly with anger and root it out from our lives. This cannot be achieved without the help of the Holy Spirit. Corrie ten Boom, involved in the Dutch Resistance and imprisoned by the Nazis in the Ravensbrück concentration camp, describes how all these three are involved in dealing with anger:

It was in a church in Munich that I saw him, a balding heavy-set man in a gray overcoat, a brown felt hat clutched between his hands. People were filing out of the basement room where I had just spoken, moving along the rows of wooden chairs to the door at the rear. It was 1947 and I had come from Holland to defeated Germany with the message that God forgives.

It was the truth they needed most to hear in that bitter, bombed-out land, and I gave them my favorite mental picture. Maybe because the sea is never far from a Hollander's mind, I liked to think that that's where forgiven sins were thrown. "When we confess our sins," I said, "God casts them into the deepest ocean, gone forever."

The solemn faces stared back at me, not quite daring to believe. There were never questions after a talk in Germany in 1947. People stood up in silence, in silence collected their coats, in silence left the room.

And that's when I saw him, working his way forward against the others. One moment I saw the overcoat and the brown hat; the next, a blue uniform and a visored cap with its skull and crossbones. It came back with a rush: the huge room with its harsh overhead lights, the pathetic pile of dresses and shoes in the center of the floor, the shame of walking naked past this man. I could see my sister's frail form ahead of me, ribs sharp beneath the parchment skin. Betsie, how thin you were!

Betsie and I had been arrested for concealing Jews in our home during the Nazi occupation of Holland; this man had been a guard at Ravensbrück concentration camp where we were sent.

Now he was in front of me, hand thrust out: "A fine message, Fräulein! How good it is to know that, as you say, all our sins are at the bottom of the sea!"

And I, who had spoken so glibly of forgiveness, fumbled in my wallet rather than take that hand. He would not remember me, of course—how could he remember one prisoner among those thousands of women?

But I remembered him and the leather crop swinging from his belt. It was the first time since my release that I had been face to face with one of my captors and my blood seemed to freeze.

"You mentioned Ravensbrück in your talk," he was saying. "I was a guard in there." No, he did not remember me.

"But since that time," he went on, "I have become a Christian. I know that God has forgiven me for the cruel things I did there, but I would like to hear it from your lips as well. Fräulein—" again the hand

57

came out—"will you forgive me?"

And I stood there—I whose sins had every day to be forgiven—and could not. Betsie had died in that place—could he erase her slow, terrible death simply for the asking?

It could not have been many seconds that he stood there, hand held out, but to me it seemed hours as I wrestled with the most difficult thing I had ever had to do.

For I had to do it—I knew that. The message that God forgives has a prior condition: that we forgive those who have injured us. "If you do not forgive men their trespasses," Jesus says, "neither will your Father in heaven forgive your trespasses."

I knew it not only as a commandment of God, but as a daily experience. Since the end of the war I had had a home in Holland for victims of Nazi brutality. Those who were able to forgive their former enemies were able also to return to the outside world and rebuild their lives, no matter what the physical scars. Those who nursed bitterness remained invalids. It was as simple and as horrible as that.

And still I stood there with the coldness clutching my heart. But forgiveness is not an emotion—I knew that too. Forgiveness is an act of the will, and the will can function regardless of the temperature of the heart. "Jesus, help me!" I prayed silently. "I can lift my hand. I can do that much. You supply the feeling."

And so woodenly, mechanically, I thrust my hand into the one stretched out to me. And as I did, an incredible thing took place. The current started in my shoulder, raced down my arm, sprang into our joined hands. And then this healing warmth seemed to flood my whole being, bringing tears to my eyes.

"I forgive you, brother!" I cried. "With all my heart!" For a long moment we grasped each other's hands, the former guard and the former prisoner. I had never known God's love so intensely as I did then. [25]

5
How to Avoid Sexual Sin
Matthew 5:27–30

[27] You have heard that it was said, "Do not commit adultery." [28] But I tell you that anyone who looks at a woman lustfully has already committed adultery with her in her heart. [29] If your right eye causes you to sin, gouge it out and throw it away. It is better for you to lose one part of your body than for your whole body to be thrown into hell. [30] And if your right hand causes you to sin, cut it off and throw it away. It is better for you to lose one part of your body than for your whole body to go into hell.

The subject of adultery is never far from the headlines. There are sometimes front-page stories of politicians who have been accused of or have even admitted to adulterous affairs. On the crime pages we frequently read of murder cases in which adultery has been a cause. Nor is the church immune. Too often there are reports of clergy, from all types of churches, who have committed adultery. Two of the biggest films of recent years, *Fatal Attraction* and *Indecent Proposal*, have centered around the subject of adultery.

Adultery appears to be on the increase. Our society puts a strong emphasis on sexual fulfillment rather than commitment to the stable institution of marriage. In 1993 in England, adultery was the "fact" proven in 44,466 divorce cases, over one quarter of the divorces for that year. Since this is probably only the tip of the iceberg, it shows the appalling scale of the problem.

In order to understand the teaching of Jesus on this subject, we need to look at the biblical view of marriage which underlies it. Marriage is one of God's greatest blessings. It brings some of the highest joys of human life. Singleness may be an even higher calling, but marriage is God's norm. Family life is the basic structure of society as God intended it to be. Within that, marriage is absolutely essential.

The Anglican wedding services summarize the purposes of marriage. First, there is the joy of companionship: "That husband and wife may comfort and help each other, living faithfully together in need and in plenty, in sorrow and in joy." [26] Secondly, it is the context for children to be brought up in an atmosphere of security and love. For the children, the relationship between the parents is even more important than the parent/child relationship. Thirdly, there is the joy of physical union: "That with delight and tenderness they may know each other in love, and through the joy of their bodily union, may strengthen the union of their hearts and lives." [27]

Sexual intercourse is "the epicenter of the personal center of marriage." [28] It is God's design that sex should cement the relationship of marriage. It brings about a union which is not just physical and biological, but emotional, psychological, spiritual, and social. It not only expresses that union, it also brings it about. "There is a tendency to think of sex as something degrading; it is not, it is magnificent, an enormous privilege, but because of that the rules are tremendously strict and severe." [29]

Adultery, which means sexual intercourse with a person who is not one's spouse, is expressly forbidden by the seventh commandment (Exodus 20:14; Deuteronomy 5:18). In the Old Testament the Mosaic penalty for adultery was stoning. It was taken so seriously because of the damage it does to marriage. It is a form of unfaithfulness which often wrecks a marriage. It is usually secretive and almost inevitably leads to somebody getting very badly hurt. Often all the parties involved are hurt, especially any children. Further, the resulting breakdown in family life is unraveling the very fabric of our society. There is an increasing relaxation of all sexual standards, but especially regarding adultery. A common attitude of those caught in adultery is: "I just couldn't help it." They are simply unable to face up to their responsibilities and exercise self-control.

While our society may question whether there is anything wrong with adultery, Jesus' teaching goes the other way. He expounds the full depth of the meaning of the command "You shall not commit adultery," and shows that this sin is not confined to the physical act during an existing marriage. It can be committed in other ways as well. In the second and third illustrations of God's standard of righteousness set out in verse 20, He calls His followers to absolute chastity outside marriage and absolute fidelity within marriage. He tells us that to fall short of these standards is to be guilty of breaking the seventh commandment. In this chapter we will look at how the seventh commandment can be broken in the heart and mind.

WHAT IS LUST? (VSS. 27–28)

Jesus intensifies and sharpens the seventh commandment. He says, "You have heard that it was said, "Do not commit adultery." But I tell you that anyone who looks at a woman lustfully has already committed adultery with her in his heart" (vs. 28). It is not that Jesus is trying to ruin our fun. Rather Jesus is warning us of the slippery slope. Edmund Burke, the eighteenth-century British statesman and political thinker, said:

> The instances are exceedingly rare of men immediately passing over a clear marked line from virtue into declared vice and corruption. There are middle tints and shades between the two extremes; there is something uncertain on the confines of the two empires which they must pass through, and which renders the change easy and imperceptible.

There has been a tendency to confine the prohibition against adultery to overt acts. As with unjust anger, which Jesus sees as the motive behind killing, so Jesus sees lust as the attitude and motive behind adultery. He is concerned not only with actions and deeds, but with thoughts and desires. Even if our conduct is outwardly moral and correct we can be guilty of adultery in our thoughts, hearts, and imaginations.

Jesus is pointing out that the chain of sin which leads ultimately to the physical act of adultery starts in the mind. The action of adultery is a symptom of a disease of the mind. If sin were not allowed in the mind it would not manifest itself in the physical act.

It is important to note that Jesus does not forbid looking at someone, rather it is looking "lustfully" which constitutes adultery in the heart. There is nothing wrong with the appreciation of a person's beauty. Nor is Jesus outlawing the natural and normal human desires which are part of our instinct and nature. We are not intended to feel guilty about the longing for personal fulfillment or the feeling of attraction toward someone else.

What Jesus is speaking against is the uncontrolled and consuming sexual passion which leads us first to contemplate adultery, and then to commit it in our mind. It is "the untamed desire for another's body."[30] It applies both to men and women, married or unmarried.

This kind of lust is well described in an article which appeared a few years ago in *Leadership Today* entitled, " 'The War Within: an Anatomy of Lust'—an anonymous Christian leader recounts his experience." It began, "I remember vividly the night I first encountered lust. Real, willful commitment to lust." He describes how he was on a trip away from home and was lured into going to see a striptease show. "Ten years have passed since that awakening, ten years never far away from the presence of lust. . . . I learned quickly that lust, like physical sex, points in only one direction. You cannot go back to a lower level and stay satisfied. . . . Lust does not satisfy; it stirs up . . . where I ended up was . . . incomprehensible to me when I started." Although he never committed the physical act of adultery, it had a subtle effect on his marriage as he began to devalue his wife as a sexual being and focus on her minor flaws. It also had a devastating effect on his spiritual life, with lust becoming the one corner of his life which God could not enter. He felt torn apart by "an overwhelming desire to be cleansed and an overwhelming desire to cling to the exotic pleasures of lust." Matters came to a head when he went to visit a pastor of a large church and finally unloaded some of the guilt he felt, only to discover that this pastor had the same problem. Indeed, he took out of his pocket a pad of paper showing the prescriptions he took to fight the venereal disease he had picked up along the way. The lawyers were already dividing up his house, his possessions and his children. [31]

Jesus warns that this kind of lust is a road that leads to hell (vss. 29–30). He is not saying that one look deserves hell. Nor is He equating thoughts and actions—clearly the act of adultery has more serious and wide-ranging consequences than simply the thought. But Jesus is warning that the process starts with our thoughts, leads to actions, and eventually to a pattern of life which could lead to hell. That is why this is such a serious business and it is so important to take great care.

HOW DO WE AVOID LUST? (VSS. 29–30)

Jesus urges us to take extreme action in order to deal with sin. His teaching applies to all sin. Nowhere does He suggest that sexual sin is the most serious of all sins, but His teaching here is put in the context of sexual sin. He says:

> If your right eye causes you to sin, gouge it out and throw it away. It is better for you to lose one part of your body than for your whole body to be thrown into hell. And if your right hand causes you to sin, cut it off and throw it away. It is better for you to lose one part of your body than for your whole body to go into hell (vss. 29–30).

Jesus did not mean us to interpret His teaching in crude literalism.

63

Origen (c. 186–255), the third-century scholar, castrated himself so that he would not be tempted. Such action was eventually forbidden by the Council of Nicea in A.D. 325. Jesus did not mean "a literal physical self-maiming, but a ruthless moral self-denial."[32] We are not to flirt with sin, but to deal drastically with it. Some of us are more prone to temptation in this area than others. We may need to examine our lives honestly and prayerfully in order to recognize where we are vulnerable, and to set ourselves responsible personal guidelines.

In particular, Jesus draws attention to three areas where great self-control is required. First, we must take control of our eyes and what we look at. Job said:

> I made a covenant with my eyes not to look lustfully at a girl. . . . If my heart has been led by my eyes, or if my hands have been defiled . . . if my heart has been enticed by a woman . . . that would have been shameful, a sin to be judged. It is a fire that burns to Destruction; it would have uprooted my harvest (Job 31:1, 7, 9, 11–12).

As C. H. Spurgeon put it, "Better a blind saint than a quick-sighted sinner."[33] In a world which is saturated with sexual stimulation we may need to take great care about the movies, TV shows, and videos that we watch, the books and magazines we read, and even the ads we look at.

It does not mean we cannot look at a beautiful person. Bishop Taylor Smith said he enjoyed looking at a pretty woman. However, he always turned his enjoyment into prayer. He thanked God for making her beautiful and prayed she would be given extra strength for the extra temptation!

Secondly, we must exercise control over how we use our hands (vs. 30). This might apply to what we pick up with our hands to read, but also to how we use our hands to touch another person. Non-sexual touch is good and healthy, although ambiguous hugs, touches, or contact can be manipulative. Sexual touching, however, is part of foreplay which is intended to lead to sexual intercourse within marriage. That is why "petting" usually leads, at best, to frustration and can lead to sin.

Thirdly, Jesus warns us of the possibility of our feet leading us into sin (Matthew 18:8). We may need to be careful of the places we go to.

For some, certain areas of town, shops and places of "entertainment" may not be conducive to sexual purity. Jesus is saying that anything which helps seduce us into sin must be ruthlessly rooted out of our lives. It is unwise to wait until we are on the brink of the physical act of adultery before we take action. The time to start is much earlier in the chain of temptation. We need to watch the friendships we make. Of course, all our lives are enriched by friendships with the opposite sex, but it is unwise for a married person to get too close to someone of the opposite sex, whether it be a co-worker, tennis partner, secretary, or confidant. Personally, I do not think it wise for men to counsel or minister to women on their own, or vice versa. I try to make it a rule that I will not pray with a woman on my own.

' A couple of hours of prayers... and then we talk more ? "

So many male Christian ministers who have fallen into adultery say that it all began because they entered a close pastoral counseling relationship with a distressed woman. My response may seem exaggerated or over-cautious, but my understanding of the teaching of Jesus is that it is worth taking extreme measures. These precautions do not stem from a lack of trust in God or our partners, but from the realization that many of us are vulnerable in this area.

Billy Graham is an example of a man who has wisely taken extreme measures in this area. In his biography, *A Prophet with Honor*, William Martin speaks of Billy Graham's "passion to be pure." He does not imagine himself or anyone else as beyond corruption. He has

long clearly understood that his best strategy for avoiding sexual temptation was to keep himself out of its path. "I'm sure I have been tempted . . .
especially in my younger years. But there has never been anything close to
an incident." How had he managed that record? "I took precautions.
From the earliest days, I have never had a meal alone with a woman other
than Ruth, not even in a restaurant. I have never ridden in an automobile
alone with a woman." Even past 70, on the rare occasions when only he
and his secretary are in a room together, he keeps the door open wide so
that none will suspect him of unseemly behavior.

On the other hand he is not a prude. On one occasion, in 1983,
he appeared in a TV show with Joan Collins. The interviewer asked,
"Billy, were you aware that Joan Collins has appeared in *Playboy*?" He
replied, "Yes, I've seen it. Someone showed it to me in the barber
shop." He then went on to preach the Gospel. On another occasion,
he mentioned that he had seen the film *Dangerous Liaisons*.

"I was staying near Times Square," he explained, "so I went to see it. It was
based in the eighteenth century in France. It was very interesting. There
were a couple of scenes which were pretty steamy. The people were about
half nude. But you could see that anywhere . . ." He seemed unworried
that someone might discover he had seen a "pretty steamy" movie without
launching a boycott of the satanic film industry. In short, he seemed to
know when he needed external controls and when he did not. Graham's
passion for sexual fidelity doubtless stems primarily from his unshakable
conviction that fidelity is God's will and infidelity a mortal sin.[34]

None of this means that we withdraw from the world. As we have
already seen, we are called to be at the center of all areas of society in
order to be the "salt" and "light" of the world. However, we must
acknowledge our weaknesses and withdraw uncompromisingly
from sin.

WHAT HAPPENS IF WE FAIL?

If the standard were merely the Pharisees' standard, many of us would be able to say that we had not broken the command "You shall not commit adultery." However, when Jesus shows us its true meaning, surely all of us become conscious of our failure. None of us can honestly say that we have never looked at someone else with lust in our hearts. So what can we do when we fail?

First, *we need to repent.* In Psalm 51 we see David's prayer of repentance. He recognized sin as sin. He did not try to justify himself or make excuses, but rather accepted responsibility and cried out for mercy. If we have been sinning in this area, we need to stop. Repentance involves turning away from what we know is wrong. We need to get rid of any magazines, videos, or other material which could prove unhelpful.

Secondly, *we need to receive forgiveness.* David, one of the greatest men of God in the Old Testament, fell in this area (2 Samuel 11–12). He did not escape the consequences of his sin, but his guilt was removed. We do not need to go on feeling guilty. David prayed for and recovered much of what he had lost. He recovered a sense of the presence of God, the power of the Spirit, the joy of his salvation, his enthusiasm for God's work, his effectiveness, and his intimacy with God.

Thirdly, *we need to resist and run.* "What makes resisting temptation difficult for many people is they don't want to discourage it completely." [35] Peter warns us: "Your enemy the devil prowls around like a roaring lion looking for someone to devour. Resist him . . ." (1 Peter 5:8). When Joseph was working for Potiphar, one of Pharaoh's officials, Potiphar's wife said to him on one occasion, "Come to bed with me!" He refused point blank and said, "How then could I do such a wicked thing and sin against God?" Although she spoke to Joseph day after day, he refused to go to bed with her or even to be with her. One day she caught him by his cloak and said,

CHAPTER 5 / HOW TO AVOID SEXUAL SIN

"Come to bed with me!" but he left his cloak in her hand and ran out of the house (Genesis 39:1–12).

Fourthly, *we need to relate.* We need to find one or two other people who will encourage us, pray with us, and ask questions. One former president of Inter-Varsity Christian Fellowship and author of best-selling Christian books, candidly admitted that he had committed adultery. He indicated that a lack of strong relationships was a major factor in his fall into sin: "I now realize that I was lacking in mutual accountability through personal relationships. We need friendships where one man regularly looks another man in the eye and asks hard questions about his moral life, his lust, his ambitions, his ego." [36]

Fifthly, *we need to recommit to Christ and His service.* We cannot escape temptation. Anthony lived a hermit's life, fasted, went without sleep, and tortured his body. For 35 years he lived in the desert and for 35 years he fought a non-stop battle. As John Wimber often says, "It is hard to sit still and be good." The best way to keep out of trouble is to get involved in Christian service.

Sixthly, *we need to be refilled.* Will-power on its own is not enough. We need the Holy Spirit's power. We are not on our own in this struggle. The apostle Paul writes, "Live by the Spirit, and you will not gratify the desires of the sinful nature" (Galatians 5:16). Elsewhere he writes this: "If by the Spirit you put to death the misdeeds of the body, you will live" (Romans 8:13). Of course, he is not referring exclusively to sexual sin, but it is included in the "desires of the sinful nature" and the "misdeeds of the body," which can only be dealt with through the Holy Spirit's power.

Seventhly, *we need to realize what we are missing out on.* Earlier I quoted from an article in *Leadership Today* titled "The War Within: an Anatomy of Lust." That article not only described the fall into lust, it also described the escape. A month after the anonymous writer's visit to the pastor, he read a book which showed him that fear and guilt would not give him the resolve he required. They only added self-hatred to his problems. Rather, he saw what he was missing by continuing to harbor lust: "I was limiting my own intimacy with God. The love He offers is so transcendent and possessing that it requires our faculties to be purified and cleansed before we can possibly contain it." His repentance involved confession to his wife who gave him forgiveness and love. Only once in the year that followed did his feet begin to slip. Then, he says, "I ran, literally ran, as fast as I could out of the district." Since dealing with lust, two things had happened. First, "I have had an experience with God that has stunned me with its depth and intimacy, an experience of an order I did not even know existed before." Secondly, the passion came back into his marriage. "My wife is again becoming an object of romance. The act of sex . . . is beginning to take on the form of mystery and transcendence and inexpressible delight that its original design must have called for." [37]

6
How to Avoid Divorce

Matthew 5:31–32; 19:3–12

[31] It has been said, "Anyone who divorces his wife must give her a certificate of divorce." [32] But I tell you that anyone who divorces his wife, except for marital unfaithfulness, causes her to become an adulteress, and anyone who marries the divorced woman commits adultery.

[3] Some Pharisees came to him to test him. They asked, "Is it lawful for a man to divorce his wife for any and every reason?"

[4] "Haven't you read," he replied, "that at the beginning the Creator 'made them male and female,' [5] and said, 'For this reason a man will leave his father and mother and be united to his wife, and the two will become one flesh'? [6] So they are no longer two, but one. Therefore what God has joined together, let man not separate."

[7] "Why then," they asked, "did Moses command that a man give his wife a certificate of divorce and send her away?"

[8] Jesus replied, "Moses permitted you to divorce your wives because your hearts were hard. But it was not this way from the beginning. [9] I tell you that anyone who divorces his wife, except for marital unfaithfulness, and marries another woman commits adultery."

[10] The disciples said to him, "If this is the situation between a husband and wife, it is better not to marry."

[11] Jesus replied, "Not everyone can accept this word, but only those to whom it has been given. [12] For some are eunuchs because they were born that way; others were made that way by men; and others have renounced marriage because of the kingdom of heaven. The one who can accept this should accept it."

Over the last 30 years there have been many forces at work in our society eating away at the family, and marriage has come increasingly under attack. As underlying causes for this situation Andrew Cornes, former Director of Training at All Souls Church here in England, lists among other things the emphasis on rights rather than duty, unrealistic expectations of easy and sustained happiness, the removal of parental support, the acceptance of divorce and remarriage, and the decline of religion. [38] Whatever the reasons, the statistics speak for themselves. In 1994 in the U.K. there were 291,069 marriages and 158,175 divorces—over half of the number of 1994 marriages.

The issue of divorce and remarriage is complex and controversial, painful and stressful. It is a vital issue for all of us. Even if it does not affect us directly, we are almost certain to know someone who is struggling with this issue. It was also a hot issue at the time of Jesus—family life stood in great danger of destruction when Christianity first came into the world. In the Greco–Roman world, although not in Judaism, relationships outside marriage were considered natural and normal. Written or oral notice in the presence of two witnesses was sufficient for a divorce. It was almost as straightforward as the Pueblo Indians today, where a woman can divorce her husband by leaving his moccasins on the doorstep!

According to Rabbinic law a man had the right to divorce his wife, but the woman had no such right to divorce her husband. All that the husband had to do was to hand the document to the woman in the presence of two witnesses and she was divorced.

As for the grounds for divorce there were two different schools of thought, revolving around the interpretation of Deuteronomy 24, which appears to allow divorce when a husband finds "something indecent" (vs. 1) about his wife. According to the strict school led by Rabbi Shammai, this meant a serious sexual offense. According to the liberal school led by Rabbi Hillel, the husband could divorce his wife "for any and every reason" (hence the question asked by the Pharisees in Matthew 19:3). This was taken to include gossiping in the street, losing her looks, having an unsightly mole, or putting too much salt in his soup. Hillel's view appears to have been the more popular with men!

In the Sermon on the Mount Jesus gives His view about divorce and remarriage and expands on this later in the Gospel (Matthew 19:3–12). The Pharisees asked Jesus, in effect, whether He agreed with Hillel's view. In this chapter I want to ask four questions arising from the teaching of Jesus.

WHAT MAKES A MARRIAGE?

There are many views today about the nature of marriage. The secular world regards it as self-chosen, self-created, and self-sustained. It is a voluntary partnership created by the decision of the two parties involved and, like any other civil contract, it can be terminated by those parties. It is often seen as a romantic alliance based on erotic attraction. If love dies, there is no reason why the marriage should not be dissolved, leaving the parties free to enter into other partnerships. Some take an increasingly reductionist view of what marriage is about. For example, John Diamond writing in *The Times* on the nature of divorce said:

Nowadays, for most people at least, marriage is one of those optional things you do if you want to make a particular sort of statement about the life you already share . . . that I share a bed and a mortgage with somebody is the substance of the relationship: the marriage certificate has turned out to be no more than a mere bureaucratic paper ornamenting seven years of my life. [39]

At the other end are those who regard marriage as indissoluble. When Jesus said, "So they are no longer two, but one" (Matthew 19:6), they take this quite literally. They hold that there is an ontological union; that is, a union of being which not only should not be broken, but cannot be broken. Augustine (354–430) took this view which is still held by the Roman Catholic Church. Hence, the Roman Catholic Church does not regard divorce, by itself, as bringing to an end a former marriage.

Jesus had the highest view of marriage. When asked about divorce, He spoke first about marriage (Matthew 19:4–6), pointing to the creation ordinance and drawing four conclusions. First, marriage involves one man and one woman for life. Secondly, it entails leaving parents. This involves a public act which breaks the links with the former family. This does not mean that the parents are never seen again. Rather, a new family unit has been formed and the husband and wife's primary responsibility and loyalty is to that new unit. Thirdly, there is a uniting and a personal commitment. The word used implies both passion and permanence. The bond is intended to be deep and lasting. Fourthly, the "two will become one flesh." Whereas leaving and uniting are active ideas, "becoming one flesh" is something that happens to the couple—they are joined by God. The union takes place at the deepest level of personality; sexual intercourse both facilitates and symbolizes this union.

Jesus summarized this teaching as meaning that in marriage, husband and wife are no longer two but one. "Therefore what God

74

has joined together, let man not separate." The fundamental rule is that marriage is permanent and divorce should be ruled out, not because marriage cannot be broken, but because it *ought* not to be broken. Separation is possible, but it is wrong. As Karl Barth once said, "To enter marriage is to renounce the possibility of leaving it."[40]

In 1991 the Law Society in England called for legislation that would enable couples to draw up legally binding marriage contracts setting out who would get what if they were to divorce: a prenuptial agreement. This is totally contrary to the Christian idea of marriage and it is hard to think of anything more undermining to this union. The possibility of divorce should be ruled out from the start. Indeed, it is wise not to let the word "divorce" enter the marriage relationship, even as a joke.

WHAT BREAKS A MARRIAGE?

The Pharisees challenged Jesus' view of marriage by quoting, or rather misquoting, Deuteronomy 24:1 (Matthew 19:7). This appears to have been quite a common misquotation, as Jesus points out: "It has been said, 'Anyone who divorces his wife must give her a certificate of divorce' " (Matthew 5:31). This misquotation readily condones divorce. The original context of Deuteronomy 24:1 was quite different. Mosaic legislation was designed to protect the wife and restrict remarriage by forbidding a husband to divorce his wife and then remarry her if his next marriage failed. In other words, if he gave his wife a divorce, it was to be permanent.

Jesus points out that the Israelites were never *commanded* to divorce their wives, even in extreme circumstances. Divorce was allowed only rarely—it was a *concession* "because your hearts were hard" (Matthew 19:8). God did not originally intend marriage to end in divorce, and declares, "I hate divorce" (Malachi 2:16).

Starting with this foundation Jesus goes on to say that divorce is the equivalent of adultery (Matthew 19:9; 5:32). He makes one exception over which there has been great debate. The one exception, appearing only in Matthew's Gospel, is "marital unfaithfulness" (vs. 9). What did He mean by this? Those who accept the authority of Scripture are divided in their interpretation. The views that I express in the rest of this chapter are my own tentative conclusions.

Some argue that the Greek word used here *(porneia)* indicates a marriage contracted within the prohibited degrees of kinship (Leviticus 18:6–18). Such a marriage would have been an illicit union and therefore no marriage at all. They take Jesus as prohibiting all divorce, which would fit the indissolublists' line.

Others take *porneia* to mean fornication before marriage, discovered afterwards. More commonly it is taken to include adultery. In both cases the penalty under Old Testament law was death (Deuteronomy 22:20–22), which under Roman law could not be enforced. Nevertheless adultery meant a new union had been formed and therefore divorce was a recognition that the marriage had already been terminated. In effect it "ratifies the rupture."[41]

Jesus is affirming the permanence of marriage. Only in the most extreme cases can a marriage be ended. Some have interpreted the teaching of Jesus with Pharisaic literalism. One act of adultery is enough to give the other partner "biblical grounds" for divorce. That is not consistent with the spirit of Jesus' teaching, nor with the rest of the New Testament. Paul, in 1 Corinthians 7, while affirming the permanence of marriage, mentions another example which ends marriage. If an unbelieving partner leaves and will not be reconciled, the believer may with clear conscience let him go. Paul would not have added a new ground unless he thought it was consistent with the broader context of Jesus' teaching. What Jesus and the rest of the New Testament confirms is that marriage is permanent, and divorce should only be allowed in the most extreme cases, where there is gross misconduct such as undermines the whole marriage relationship. For example, if one party leaves and sets up home with another and has children by that new partner and will not return to their spouse, in effect adultery has ended the first marriage. If an unbelieving partner leaves and will not be reconciled, the believer has to let him go. Another extreme case could be if someone is on the receiving end of physical or mental abuse. In these cases there is no other option.

Jesus' teaching, which is more like that of Shammai than that of Hillel, causes a strong reaction in His disciples: "If this is the situation between a husband and wife, it is better not to marry" (Matthew 19:10). They were surprised by His strictness. But Jesus knew the damage done by divorce. Tearing apart what God has joined together will inevitably cause great damage at least to one of the partners and probably to both. Further, if there are children, they are bound to be seriously affected, perhaps for life.

In 1995 the National Child Development Survey showed results of research based on 17,000 children born in Britain in 1958. Those children whose parents had divorced were, on average, less emotionally stable, left home earlier, and divorced or separated more frequently themselves. They showed more behavioral problems in school, were more likely to be unhappy and worried, and were twice as likely to have a child before the age of 20. Children born to middle-class parents who divorced had twice the chance of leaving school without any qualifications and were much less likely to secure a full-time job.

IS IT EVER RIGHT FOR DIVORCED CHRISTIANS TO REMARRY?

Some say that although Jesus allowed divorce in the case of adultery, He did not allow remarriage. This is based on the view that the first marriage is indissoluble until the death of one of the parties. However, this view has several difficulties. First, although Deuteronomy 24:1–4 does not encourage divorce and remarriage, it does contemplate the possibility. Marriage, in the Old Testament, is not regarded as indissoluble.

Secondly, in the society of Jesus' day it was generally assumed that divorced people would remarry. Hence Jesus says that anyone who divorces his wife "causes her to become an adulteress" (Matthew 5:32). Clearly this would not be the case if she remained single. But the woman had little option. In a society with no social security and no paid jobs for women, financial constraints forced her to remarry or become a prostitute. Practically all cultures in the ancient world understood that divorce carried with it the permission to remarry.

Thirdly, those who take the indissolublists' line end up with an inconsistent position. Taking their position to its logical conclusion would mean that if a person became a Christian and he had previously married, divorced, remarried and had children, that person should leave his new spouse and children and return to his former spouse. They say, "You should see that your present marriage is now God's will for you." [42] Another wrote:

> The new couple have entered into a marriage covenant. They should not have done so, but they have; and that covenant is now binding on them. They cannot repudiate it at will; they should not repudiate it, even if they subsequently realize it was a mistake (cf. Ecclesiastes 5:4–7). Therefore it is entirely right that Christians should pray for a second marriage that has run into difficulties to be sustained. [43]

This is illogical if the first marriage was indissoluble.

Even if divorce ends a marriage legally and morally, this does not mean that for Christians today remarriage should be taken for granted for everyone. Even if the partners are free to remarry, in some cases it may not be right to do so. It might be that God calls a particular person to witness to the permanence of marriage by not remarrying.

Bearing all this in mind, the question of whether a remarriage should take place in a church is very difficult. The church has a dual role. First, it has a prophetic role to witness to the permanence of marriage. Secondly, it has a pastoral role to witness to the possibility of forgiveness and a new start. The approach of the Anglican Church is normally to disallow remarriage in church, but in appropriate cases to hold a service of blessing after the civil wedding. Although different views are possible, perhaps the Anglican solution is an appropriate way of bearing witness to both these roles.

HOW ARE WE TO RESPOND?

For those who are *already divorced*, in one sense it is obviously too late, especially if one or both of the former partners have remarried. Here, the giving and receiving of forgiveness is the key. Almost invariably, to some degree, both parties are to blame for the divorce. It is vitally important to repent where necessary. This may mean asking a former partner to forgive and not to carry bitterness, anger, and resentment. This is likely to be an ongoing process. Even more common is a sense of guilt and failure and here it is vital to receive forgiveness. Divorce is not an unforgivable sin. Jesus died to set us free from guilt. It is important to accept that the marriage is over, that in Christ the guilt can be removed, and that there is now a freedom to start again. This does not mean that remarriage is necessarily right, but it is not necessarily wrong.

For those who are *married*, it is essential to do all that we can to avoid divorce. Even if the process of divorce has begun, it is never too late. In Christ, there is no such thing as irretrievable breakdown. If your partner is seeking to divorce you, it is important to explore every possibility of reconciliation. Reconciliation is always possible, even at the very last minute. [44]

If you are in the process of divorcing your partner, think again. Even those who have been at the receiving end of gross misconduct should still be willing to seek reconciliation. How long this process will go on will vary from case to case. Talk to somebody about it and consider whether there is not some way that reconciliation could be possible.

If you are not yet at that stage, but your marriage is experiencing difficulties, get help early. Too often people find it hard to acknowledge that their marriage is under pressure. Don't wait until there is a crisis. Take advantage of courses and weekends aimed at strengthening marriage.

All of us who are married need to build strong marriages. We need to see it as the highest priority of our lives, after our relationship with God. We must avoid succumbing to the temptation of putting our work or our children before our marriage partner.

Strong marriages are built by regular and intimate communication, which increases friendship, trust, and mutual respect. More relationships break down through lack of communication than any other reason. Communication takes time and this needs to be built into our marriage.

".. So what do you do for a living?"

We are put under great pressure, both from our society whose values are not those of Jesus Christ, and from the devil whose aim is to steal, kill, and destroy. It is sometimes said, "If the grass is greener on the other side of the fence it is time to start watering your own." Strong marriages always require attention and are sustained by prayer. Couples must find time to pray together and separately for their relationship.

Those who are *unmarried* need to see singleness not as a curse but as a blessing, as an opportunity to accomplish much in life without distractions and the inevitable giving of time and energy to a spouse and family. Certainly, it is better to be single than to be unhappily married. It is also worth stressing, though it may seem obvious, that great care needs to be taken over the choice of a marriage partner (see *Questions of Life*, Chapter 7).

We need to model strong marriages to the world. Many don't have many models of a good marriage. The most powerful witness to Christ is the different quality of our lives, our relationships, and especially our marriages. We also need to draw alongside those facing marriage problems with compassion and understanding, without being judgmental.

The heart of the Gospel is reconciliation. God in Christ reconciled the world to Himself. Our task is to proclaim this message to the world. We do it by our lives, by our example in our relationships, and by our lips, proclaiming Jesus' teaching to the world, seeking to reconcile people to God and to each other. When the church truly starts living out the teaching of Jesus, then the world will take notice and will have a chance to respond.

7
How to Live and Act with Integrity
Matthew 5:33–37

[33] Again, you have heard that it was said to the people long ago, "Do not break your oath, but keep the oaths you have made to the Lord." [34] But I tell you, Do not swear at all: either by heaven, for it is God's throne; [35] or by the earth, for it is his footstool; or by Jerusalem, for it is the city of the Great King. [36] And do not swear by your head, for you cannot make even one hair white or black. [37] Simply let your "Yes" be "Yes," and your "No," "No"; anything beyond this comes from the evil one.

We recently returned from a week away to find a man outside our house who claimed to be one of our next door neighbor's cousins. He told us that his car with all his belongings inside had been towed and he needed to pay a fine in order to get it back. He asked if he could borrow some money, so we gave him $50. He returned a little later saying that he needed another $20. Having lent him this, we suddenly became suspicious. I went to our neighbors' house and saw that all the lights were on. I knew I had been conned. It turned out that the man was a drug addict and had used the same story to deceive many people in the neighborhood.

I realized what a gullible idiot I had been. But I also thought how sad it was that we live in a world where we cannot trust people.

Lynda Lee-Potter writing in the *Daily Mail* reported:

> The *Sun* newspaper recently conducted a "truth searching survey" to find out more about the minds, hearts, and integrity of its readers. It purported to be ecstatic to find only 22% of them would kill a partner for cash, and a mere 38% of men would let their wives earn money as a prostitute.

"Congratulations" blazed the caring *Sun*, "We have always known it, but now we have the evidence. You *Sun* readers are decent, honest, caring, and trustworthy. You are loyal workers, faithful lovers, caring members of the community." "Except," they should perhaps have added, "those of you who are potential pimps or murderers."[45]

We live in a world rife with deception. Dishonesty abounds. The crime rate is soaring. The majority of offenses are related to dishonesty: burglary, fraud, or theft. However, it is obviously not only in the criminal world where dishonesty is to be found.

There is a perception that even in many of the great institutions of the country or elsewhere, it can no longer be said with confidence that a person's word is his bond. The lies of politicians are infamous. For example, George Bush's election promise not to raise taxes was accompanied by the immortal words, "Read my lips." Yet his promise was not kept.

Because there is so much dishonesty, lawyers are brought in to draw up water-tight contracts to hold people to their word. Yet today even lawyers are not trusted and are themselves mocked when talking about honesty. Conscience has been defined as, "What a lawyer puts away from Monday to Friday and takes out again on the weekend."

The press are not known for their accuracy. Their values are speed and profit, more than accuracy and truth. "You can't trust anything in the newspapers except the date," is a common expression.

Other occupations suffer from a similar lack of credibility. Real estate agents are not often seen as honest and truthful. Used car salesmen do not have a reputation for scrupulous accuracy. Equally, they would claim that the public does not always tell them the truth when selling cars to them.

Nor is the artistic world any better. A friend of mine who worked in the record business told me that when asked where a record got to in the charts people always exaggerate. You would be expected to say "to number 30" if it got to 70. The hearer makes the necessary adjustment in his own mind.

This lack of trust extends also to personal relationships. In *Life and How to Survive It,* John Cleese and his therapist, Robin Skynner, have an interesting discussion about the human tendency to break promises. They conclude that one part of us makes a promise and another part breaks it. After the promise is made our mood alters, our circumstances change and so the promise becomes an inconvenience. This can be seen in smaller and larger ways: the schoolchild may betray a secret, and an adult may break a marriage vow.

At other times, the reason for breaking a promise is less complex—people are simply dishonest. Children make promises accompanied by oaths such as, "I swear on the Holy Bible," or, "Cross my heart and hope to die, stick a needle in my eye." Yet by common custom they can break such a promise by the simple device of having their fingers crossed behind their backs. This means you can renege on your vow with impunity. Many of these young people seem to grow up with their fingers permanently crossed behind their backs.

The society into which Jesus was speaking was just as dishonest. Having dealt with the sixth commandment (vss. 21–26) and the seventh commandment (vss. 27–32), Jesus then turns back to cover the third commandment (vss. 33–37). Once again He gives a practical example of how Christians are to live righteous lives and to be salt and light in society. This time it is by integrity, honesty, and truthfulness.

INTEGRITY WAS PART OF GOD'S PLAN FOR SOCIETY (VS. 33)

Jesus says, "Again, you have heard that it was said to the people long ago, 'Do not break your oath, but keep the oaths you have made to the Lord' " (vs. 33). This is not a quote from the Old Testament but it is an accurate summary of the Old Testament teaching on the subject of oath-taking. God allowed people to make vows using His name to reinforce their commitment, but once made, such vows had to be kept. The Old Testament prohibited all false swearing and perjury. The intention was to stop lying and to prevent the chaos caused when people can't rely on another's words. So important was the principle that it was enshrined in the third commandment, "You shall not misuse the name of the LORD your God, for the LORD will not hold anyone guiltless who misuses his name" (Exodus 20:7; Deuteronomy 5:11).

Further teaching on the subject is found in the rest of the Pentateuch (the first five books of the Old Testament): "Do not steal. Do not lie. Do not deceive one another. Do not swear falsely by my name and so profane the name of your God. I am the LORD" (Leviticus 19:11–12) and, "When a man makes a vow to the LORD or takes an oath to obligate himself by a pledge, he must not break his word but must do everything he said" (Numbers 30:2). A person was generally not required to take an oath, but if he did he had to keep it.

> If you make a vow to the LORD your God, do not be slow to pay it, for the LORD your God will certainly demand it of you and you will be guilty of sin. But if you refrain from making a vow, you will not be guilty. Whatever your lips utter you must be sure to do, because you made your vow freely to the LORD your God with your own mouth (Deuteronomy 23:21–23).

However, on some occasions oaths were actually commanded to be made (Numbers 5:19). In the rest of the Old Testament there are further references to the need to keep such vows: "Fulfill your vows to the Most High" (Psalm 50:14) and, "When you make a vow to God, do not delay in fulfilling it. He has no pleasure in fools; fulfill your vow. It is better not to vow than to make a vow and not fulfill it" (Ecclesiastes 5:4–5).

Behind all God's law is the desire of a loving God to create a society in which it would be a joy to live. If the three commands to which Jesus refers in these verses (vss. 21–37) were kept, there would be no wars, no defense budget, no divorce, no adultery, no keys, no burglar alarms, and everyone could trust their husbands and wives, neighbors, business partners, employees, employers, and everyone else. It would be a society in which politicians could be trusted and there would hardly be a need for lawyers.

Integrity involves everything we do and say (vss. 34–36). God's commands were intended to avoid perjury. The Pharisees built an entire legalistic system around the Old Testament laws. They made a distinction between vows: some were binding and some were not. Formulas which included the divine name were binding, but a person did not need to be so careful if the divine name was not involved. Like children crossing their fingers behind their backs, the Pharisees managed to find a way to avoid binding commitments.

This system of evading God's law reached its climax in a discussion which can be seen in the Jewish law where one whole section is given over to a discussion about oaths. The idea was that if God's name was used He was a party to the transaction. If not, He had nothing to do with it. Oaths by "heaven" or "earth" were not binding on witnesses. According to one rabbi, oaths "toward Jerusalem" were binding, but oaths "by Jerusalem" were not. Thus evasive swearing became a justification for lying. Instead of inspiring integrity, oaths became a breeding ground for corruption. Instead of reinforcing promises, oaths provided loopholes for people to break their commitment without repercussions. [46]

Jesus confronts this whole system of oath-taking. He points out that it is not a question of bringing God in; you cannot keep Him out. He is already there. Everything comes back to God in the end. Jesus quotes the Old Testament to show that heaven is God's throne and earth is his footstool (vss. 34–35; Isaiah 66:1) and Jerusalem is the city of the Great King (vs. 35; Psalm 48:2). Even our head, which might be thought to be a person's absolute possession, belongs to God. He decides the color of our hair (vs. 36).

Later on in Matthew's Gospel He deals again with the same issue, saying to the scribes and Pharisees:

> Woe to you, blind guides! You say, "If anyone swears by the temple, it means nothing; but if anyone swears by the gold of the temple, he is bound by his oath." You blind fools! Which is greater: the gold, or the temple that makes the gold sacred? You also say, "If anyone swears by the altar, it means nothing; but if anyone swears by the gift on it, he is bound by his oath." You blind men! Which is greater: the gift, or the altar that makes the gift sacred? Therefore, he who swears by the altar swears by it and by everything on it. And he who swears by the temple swears by it and by the one who dwells in it. And he who swears by heaven swears by God's throne and by the one who sits on it (Matthew 23:16–22).

Whether or not God is named is irrelevant, because He is there. No oath can be avoided. Life cannot be divided into compartments—those where God is involved and those where He is not. There is not one language for church and another for the workplace. God is involved in all our activities and speech. He hears every word we utter, whether it is addressed to Him or not. Our words and our lives should be consistent, whether we are in church or out of church. We cannot bring God into our transactions any more than we can keep Him out. All promises are sacred since they are all made in the presence of God.

INTEGRITY IS A MARK OF CHRISTIAN DISCIPLESHIP (VS. 37)

Jesus does not abolish the law, but in His radical teaching on integrity, He goes back to the original purpose behind the law. That purpose was to ensure truthfulness. Since the whole system of oath-taking had become corrupt and was being used to avoid telling the truth, He forbids all oaths. He says, "Do not swear at all. . . . Simply let your 'Yes' be 'Yes,' and your 'No,' 'No'; anything beyond this comes from the evil one" (vss. 34, 37).

Jesus' brother James taught something very similar in what is probably the oldest letter in the New Testament. He wrote: "Above all, my brothers, do not swear—not by heaven or by earth or by anything else. Let your 'Yes' be yes, and your 'No,' no, or you will be condemned" (James 5:12). Honest people do not need to resort to oaths.

> Clement of Alexandria insisted that Christians must lead such a life and demonstrate such a character that no one will ever dream of asking an oath from them. The ideal society is one in which no man's word will ever need an oath to guarantee its truth, and no man's promise ever need an oath to guarantee its fulfilling. [47]

I remember how my father used to say, "I expect to be believed." He regarded honesty as the highest possible value and went to absurd lengths to retain that standard. On one occasion, he and my mother got on the wrong bus, and thus got off without paying a fare. My father sent the $.25 to the bus company, but they sent it back. This resulted in a long correspondence, which my mother found hard to understand. Later, he conducted a similar exchange with British Rail when, for a different reason, he felt he owed them money. Unfortunately, their accounting system could not cope with the money he had sent.

Jesus tells His disciples simply to speak the truth on every occasion. We are to cut out all finger crossing: yes must be yes and no must be no. To add anything else is unnecessary. Indeed, "anything beyond this comes from the evil one" (vs. 37). The Greek word for "the evil one" could be translated simply "evil." It is a result of sinful human nature and wickedness in the world. Equally, it can be translated as "evil personified." It comes from the "evil one," the devil himself who is the "father of lies" (John 8:44). With these words Jesus abolished the whole oath-taking system: it would no longer be an instrument of evil to give people a loophole to avoid telling the truth.

Does this mean that all oaths and vows are prohibited to the Christian? C. H. Spurgeon, writing his commentary on these verses, argued that a Christian should not take an oath, even in court. "Christians should not yield to an evil custom, however great the pressure put upon them; but they should abide by the plain and unmistakable command of their Lord and King."[48] The Quakers have traditionally taken the same line.

However, it is not necessary to take the words of Jesus so literally as to exclude an oath in a court of law. Jesus Himself responded to the oath of testimony at His trial (Matthew 26:63–64). Paul used solemn expressions to appeal to God (2 Corinthians 1:23; Galatians 1:20; 1 Thessalonians 5:27). The author of Hebrews wrote, "Men swear by someone greater than themselves, and the oath confirms what is said and puts an end to all argument. Because God wanted to make the unchanging nature of His purpose very clear to the heirs of what was promised, He confirmed it with an oath" (Hebrews 6:16–17). The author could not have used this argument if he had thought that oaths were sinful in themselves. Jesus is not outlawing, for example, the marriage vows. These are solemn vows which invoke God's name to underscore the commitment to the marriage.

We must not be pedantic in our interpretation of the words of Jesus, lest we fall into the same trap as the Pharisees. They took too literal an approach to God's words in the Old Testament and failed to see that what lay behind the commands was the need for honesty, truthfulness, and reliability. The same desire lies behind Jesus' words as once again He goes back to the spirit and intention behind the Old Testament law.

The thrust of Jesus' words is that we should be people who keep our word. Jesus said, "I am the . . . truth" (John 14:6). Christians should be known for their truthfulness, reliability, and trustworthiness in their homes, personal relationships, and work.

I once knew a godly man nicknamed "Gibbo" who when he was young worked as a clerk at Selfridges, a department store in London. One day, when the owner Gordon Selfridge was there, the telephone rang and Gibbo answered it. The caller asked to speak to Gordon Selfridge. Gibbo passed on the message and Selfridge replied, "Tell him I'm out." Gibbo held out the receiver to him and said, "You tell him you're out." Gordon Selfridge took the call, but was furious with Gibbo. Gibbo replied: "If I can lie for you, I can lie to you." From that moment onward Gordon Selfridge had the highest regard for and trust in Gibbo.

Christians are called to be different from the society around. We are called to have a righteousness that "surpasses that of the Pharisees and the teachers of the law" (Matthew 5:20). If we do so, we will be salt and light in society (Matthew 5:13–16).

Dietrich Bonhoeffer was one of the German Christians who opposed Hitler. His integrity cost him his life. He was murdered by the Nazis shortly before the end of the war. In his commentary on these verses he wrote:

> Only those who follow Jesus and cleave to Him are living in complete truthfulness. Such men have nothing to hide from their Lord. . . . Complete truthfulness is only possible where sin has been uncovered, and forgiven by Jesus. . . . The cross is God's truth about us, and therefore it is the only power which can make us truthful. When we know the cross we are no longer afraid of the truth. We need no more oaths to confirm the truth of our utterances, for we live in the perfect truth of God.

> There is no truth towards Jesus without truth towards man. Untruthfulness destroys fellowship, but truth cuts false fellowship to pieces and establishes genuine brotherhood. [49]

8
How to Respond to Evil People

Matthew 5:38–42

³⁸ You have heard that it was said, "Eye for eye, and tooth for tooth." ³⁹ But I tell you, Do not resist an evil person. If someone strikes you on the right cheek, turn to him the other also. ⁴⁰ And if someone wants to sue you and take your tunic, let him have your cloak as well. ⁴¹ If someone forces you to go one mile, go with him two miles. ⁴² Give to the one who asks you, and do not turn away from the one who wants to borrow from you.

We have seen how Jesus' teaching requires a radical transformation in our attitude and behavior toward others, but this does not guarantee a similar transformation in their behavior toward us. However lovingly we act, there will always be people who hurt us.

In those situations, how do we respond when wronged by another person? How do we feel when insulted or when someone is rude to us? What is our response when our property or possessions are stolen or damaged by a burglary or car crash, or when someone robs us of our time or causes us a lot of time-wasting irritation? What should we do or say when we lose money due to someone else's fraud, theft or negligence?

Jesus makes the most extraordinary demand of His disciples. He tells them, "Do not resist an evil person" (vs. 39). What does this mean? Does it mean that all Christians should be pacifists? Or could it mean that we should never go to court if we are wronged? Should we submit to oppressive employers? Should we give money to everyone who approaches us in the street?

Some have taken the words of Jesus absolutely literally. Martin Luther describes the crazy saint "who let the lice nibble at him and refused to kill any of them on account of this text, maintaining that he had to suffer and could not resist evil." [50]

The nineteenth-century novelist Leo Tolstoy, toward the end of his life, took this passage absolutely literally. He believed there should not only be no soldiers, but also no police, no magistrates and no law courts. He opposed organized government because it maintained itself through coercion, and he condemned private property because he believed that ownership was secured by force. He opted out of the world altogether and ended his life pathetically alone. His writings on the subject had great influence on Gandhi, who believed in total pacifism. Even today some Christians, like the Mennonites, opt out of almost all social control for reasons based largely on this section of the Sermon on the Mount.

At the other extreme is the atheist philosopher Friedrich Nietzsche, notorious for his claim that "God is dead," who totally rejected this teaching of Jesus. He contended that Jesus' words were proof of the fact that Christianity was for the weak and cowardly. He regarded it as a slave morality where charity, humility, and obedience replaced competition, pride, and autonomy. His search for a "superman," perfected in both mental and physical strength and without moral scruples, was later taken up and adapted by Adolf Hitler.

So just how should this section of the Sermon on the Mount be interpreted? We need to look at what was taught on this subject in the Old Testament and then we need to look at what Jesus taught and how both should be interpreted and applied.

WHAT DID THE OLD TESTAMENT TEACH? (VS. 38)

When Jesus said, "You have heard that it was said . . ." He was usually referring to scribal additions and subtractions. Here He is quoting directly from the Old Testament itself, and once again He is attacking the scribal misinterpretation and wrong application of the Old Testament text.

"An eye for an eye and a tooth for a tooth" is the oldest law in the world. It is known as the *lex talionis*, which means essentially the law of "tit for tat." It was part of the civil law of Israel and is quoted three times in the Old Testament (Exodus 21:23–25; Leviticus 24:19–20; Deuteronomy 19:21). Even earlier than that it was part of the code of Hammurabi, who reigned in Babylon 2288–2242 B.C. The actual code probably dates from the eighteenth century B.C. and is one of the earliest known codes of law. The code of Hammurabi made a distinction in the punishments for an offense against a gentleman (eye for eye) and offenses against a poor man (monetary penalties). The Old Testament law made no such distinctions.

HOW SHOULD THE OLD TESTAMENT HAVE BEEN INTERPRETED AND APPLIED?

William Barclay, in his commentary on this section, draws attention to four qualifications in relation to the Old Testament law. First, in the Old Testament, this law was intended to be a law of mercy; it was restrictive rather than permissive. The legal punishment was not to exceed the gravity of the crime, but was designed to rule out escalating revenge and replace the unlimited excesses of blood feuds. These feuds were characteristic of early society. If one member of a tribe was injured by a member of another tribe, all members of the offended tribe would take vengeance on all members of the offending tribe. This law was intended to rule out such vendettas. Instead, there was to be exact correspondence and compensation.

This is still a valid legal principle. It prevents an escalation such as: "I hit you on the nose. You cut off my hand. I kill you. Your brother kills me and my family." In May, 1989 Ali Akbar Rafsanjani, speaker of the Iranian parliament, advocated killing five citizens of the United States, a British citizen and a Frenchman for every Iranian killed. It is such escalation that the Old Testament law was designed to avert, by defining justice and restraining revenge.

Secondly, the law was clearly created for judges and not for private individuals. "The judges must make a thorough investigation.... You must purge the evil from among you ... life for life, eye for eye, tooth for tooth, hand for hand, foot for foot" (Deuteronomy 19:18–21). It was a guide for judges in sentencing. There was to be an exact correspondence in compensation. It was never intended that individuals should exact such revenge.

Thirdly, it was almost certainly never taken literally, except in the case of capital offenses. Penalties were generally replaced by financial fines and damages. The Jewish law[51] laid down how the damages are to be assessed. In a similar way to damages under the British legal system today, damages were awarded for the injury itself, for pain suffered, for medical expenses and loss of wages.

Fourthly, this was not the whole picture as far as the Old Testament was concerned. Individuals were taught not to seek revenge and not to bear grudges. Rather, they were taught, "Love your neighbor as yourself" (Leviticus 19:18). "Do not say, 'I'll do to him as he has done to me; I'll pay that man back for what he did' " (Proverbs 24:29).

Indeed, they were specifically taught, "Let him offer his cheek to one who would strike him" (Lamentations 3:30).

WHAT DID JESUS TEACH? (VSS. 39–42)

By the time of Jesus, the Old Testament law "eye for eye, tooth for tooth," designed to prevent escalation, was being used to justify personal vendettas, leading to bitterness, vengeance, malice, and hatred. The interpreters had turned a restraining injunction into a retributive one. Jesus repudiates such a misinterpretation and application. In doing so He is not repealing the law, but fulfilling it to the very last (see Matthew 5:17–20).

Jesus says, "Do not resist an evil person," i.e., one who wishes to do you injury. He forbids revenge. More than that, He forbids an unforgiving and vengeful spirit. We are not to stand on our rights, and in fact it is questionable whether we should talk in terms of "rights" at all. Jesus gives four concrete examples of non-retaliation, all of which involve an individual's response to loss at the hands of another.

First, Jesus gives an example of *loss of pride*. "If someone strikes you on the right cheek, turn to him the other also" (vs. 39). According to Jewish rabbinic law, a backhanded slap (on the right cheek) was twice as insulting as one with the flat of the hand (on the left). Even today in the Middle East a slap in the face is regarded as a particularly insulting assault, a gesture of extreme abuse, showing the greatest possible contempt for someone. Jesus Himself endured such assaults on more than one occasion (Mark 14:65; John 18:22; 19:3).

Billy Bray, the nineteenth-century Cornish miner and evangelist, had been a very good fighter before his conversion. Soon afterward, a fellow miner who had lived in terror of Billy Bray before Bray's conversion, made the most of his opportunity after it. He hit him without any provocation. Billy Bray could easily have laid him out unconscious but instead he looked at him and said, "May God forgive you, even as I forgive you." The result was that after several days of agony of mind and spirit, the man was converted.

Of course, we all know our pride can be hurt without physical violence. Jesus was called a glutton and a drunkard. The early Christians were accused of cannibalism (eating the body of Christ) and immorality. Although the circumstances today are different, we are not called to seek revenge, but to follow their example and "turn the other cheek."

Secondly, Jesus turns to *loss of possessions*. "And if someone wants to sue you and take your tunic, let him have your cloak as well" (vs. 40). Losing a tunic, which was the inner garment, would not have been a desperate matter, as even the poorest man would have had more than one. A cloak was more valuable and essential. Most would have had only one and used it as a robe by day and a blanket by night. It was a man's inalienable possession (Exodus 22:26; Deuteronomy 24:13). Thus Jesus encourages us not only to give up inessentials without opposition, but to add even that which we consider essential.

Jesus again teaches non-retaliation, even where our legal rights have been infringed and our possessions or property taken. We are not to think in terms of rights, but of duties. We are to have an unselfish attitude about our rights and property. As Spurgeon wrote, "Better lose a suit of cloth than be drawn into a suit in law."[52]

Thirdly, Jesus gave an example of *loss of time*. "If someone forces you to go one mile, go with him two miles" (vs. 41). The Romans, as an occupying power, used to compel citizens to supply food or carry baggage for them. If a citizen felt the touch of a Roman spear on his shoulder he knew he was about to be compelled to carry baggage for a thousand paces (slightly less than a mile), a form of service which was obviously regarded as unreasonable and hateful. It was under this custom that Simon of Cyrene was compelled to carry Jesus' cross (Matthew 27:32).

Jesus taught that we are not to respond to such evil with a vengeful attitude, but to offer to do even more. It is difficult to think of a modern equivalent. Perhaps we can begin to get the sense of infuriation that such action would be likely to cause, if we imagine how we would feel if our car was wrongly towed away to an impound lot minutes before we were due to drive to an important meeting.

Fourthly, Jesus gives an example of *loss of money*: "Give to the one who asks you, and do not turn away from the one who wants to borrow from you" (vs. 42). In the Old Testament, generosity to the poor was taught:

> If there is a poor man among your brothers in any of the towns of the land that the LORD your God is giving you, do not be hardhearted or tight-fisted toward your poor brother. Rather be openhanded and freely lend him whatever he needs. . . . Give generously to him and do so without a grudging heart; then because of this the LORD your God will bless you in all your work and in everything you put your hand to. There will always be poor people in the land. Therefore I command you to be openhanded toward your brothers and toward the poor and needy in your land (Deuteronomy 15:7–8, 10–11).

Jesus goes even further than this, teaching us to say "no" to any kind of tightfisted, penny-pinching attitudes; to put the needs of others before our convenience; and to be willing to suffer financial loss in the service of others who will never pay us back.

HOW SHOULD THE TEACHING OF JESUS BE INTERPRETED AND APPLIED?

We must not fall into the same error as the Pharisees. They had interpreted the teaching in this area in a very literal way which became legalistic. They had failed to look at the spirit behind the law, and they were not looking at it in the context of the Old Testament as a whole. Jesus is not teaching a new set of literalistic rules, but teaching a new attitude. To interpret this passage with wooden literalism would be to do exactly what Jesus speaks against;

it would be to exalt the letter at the expense of principle. It is the attitude of our hearts that matters—it would be possible to turn the other cheek in a most provocative manner. Sometimes the proponents of total pacifism act in a spirit which is far removed from the one Jesus taught.

Further, to interpret it absolutely literally would be contrary to common sense. This was not intended to be a charter for every thug, con-man, bully, and beggar. It would be quite absurd to suggest that no evil person should ever be resisted. Should women submit to rapists? Should we allow ourselves to be murdered, if the occasion arises? The illustrations which Jesus gives are illustrations of the law of love. The Christian is not "a doormat . . . rather the strong man whose control of himself and love for others are so powerful that he rejects absolutely every conceivable form of retaliation." [53]

Most important of all, to interpret it totally literally would be contrary to the life and teaching of Jesus and the rest of the New Testament. John tells us that Jesus Himself made a whip out of cords and drove the money changers from the temple area. He scattered their coins, overturned their tables and ordered them out (John 2:13–16). He stood up to the hypocrisy of the scribes and Pharisees and verbally assaulted them (e.g., Matthew 23). He demanded an explanation when struck by an official of the high priest (John 18:23).

Likewise, the apostle Paul refused to allow the authorities at Philippi to get away with beating Silas and him illegally (Acts 16:37). On other occasions he appealed to his right as a Roman citizen not to be flogged without a guilty verdict against him (Acts 22:25) and enforced his right to a trial before Caesar (Acts 25:8–12).

Further, Paul in his teaching makes a clear distinction between the dealings of the state and personal morality. The governing authorities are established by God. The one in authority is "God's servant to do you good. But if you do wrong, be afraid, for he does not bear the sword for nothing. He is God's servant, an agent of wrath to bring punishment on the wrongdoer" (Romans 13:4).

Paul's teaching does not contradict Jesus'; rather it complements it. Moreover, in relation to our personal morality, Paul's attitude is exactly like that of his master: "Do not repay anyone evil for evil. . . . Live at peace with everyone. . . . Do not take revenge" (Romans 12:17–19). The principle of love lies behind both. The state is concerned with the protection of others. To stand by and allow murder and violence would be unloving and un-Christian.

By analogy, if it is right for the authorities to use force to protect citizens against internal threats, it is equally right to use force against external ones. As Thomas Aquinas put it, "Just as they use the sword in lawful defense against domestic disturbance when they punish criminals . . . so they lawfully use the sword of war to protect from foreign attacks." Our duty as citizens may involve us in the use of force to restrain evil people. A Christian soldier may need to kill in the course of his duty. A Christian police officer may be required to use force in performing her duty. A Christian judge may be required to send people to prison. All of us as Christian citizens may be required to use force to restrain evil and to protect others. If we see a child being attacked and abused we are not to stand by idly. The principle of love requires us to interfere with force if necessary.

There is bound to be a tension within all of us. We are all private individuals with a command from Jesus not to retaliate or take revenge. We are also citizens of the state with a duty to prevent crime and bring wrongdoers to justice. If we are the victim of a crime we should forgive the criminal, not seek revenge, and yet do all in our power to bring the perpetrator of the crime to justice. It is not easy to hold this tension, but the principle of an attitude of love requires that we do so.

The same applies to civil wrongs perpetrated against us. It is not wrong to go to court, provided our motive is love and justice, not retaliation and revenge. Likewise, an evil and oppressive employer may need stopping in his tracks, but we must ensure that our motives are right. Similarly, it is not the most loving thing to give money to those whom we know will use it to abuse their own bodies with alcohol or drugs. We must ensure we do not refuse to give simply because we are not prepared for financial loss. The test may be whether we are willing to spare the time to go and buy them food to eat.

We must feel the challenge of the words of Jesus and not allow His words to die the death of a thousand qualifications. We must never allow ourselves to be motivated by revenge or malice. Rather we are to be peaceful, willing, generous, and liberal with our time, money, and resources. We are called to disregard totally our own rights and combine this with a passionate concern for the rights of others. A readiness to harbor bitterness, a quickness in taking offense, a quarrelsome and contentious disposition, and an alacrity in asserting our own rights are all contrary to the teaching of Jesus.

One man who, in many ways, followed this example was Martin Luther King, Jr. He endured unjust suffering as leader of the mass civil rights movement in the United States from the 1950s until his assassination. He did more than anyone else to break the appalling segregation laws. Dr. Benjamin Mays said this at King's funeral:

> If any man knew the meaning of suffering, King knew. House bombed; living day by day for 13 years under constant threats of death; maliciously accused of being a Communist; falsely accused of being insincere; stabbed by a member of his own race; slugged in a hotel lobby; jailed over 20 times; occasionally deeply hurt because friends betrayed him—and yet this man had no bitterness in his heart, no rancor in his soul, no revenge in his mind; and he went up and down the length and breadth of this world preaching non-violence and the redemptive power of love. [54]

We are called to live a totally different lifestyle from that of the world around us. We are called to be salt and light in our society. "To return evil for good is devilish; to return good for good is human; to return good for evil is divine." [55]

Once again Jesus takes the Old Testament law to an even deeper level. He does not supersede the Old Testament requirements; rather, He shows His disciples the true meaning of the law. He calls His disciples to suffering love in the face of evil. By His own example on the cross He showed how only such an attitude can ultimately triumph over evil. Dietrich Bonhoeffer powerfully makes the point, "It looked as though evil had triumphed on the cross, but the real victory belonged to Jesus. . . . The cross is the only power in the world which proves that suffering love can avenge and vanquish evil."[56]

9
How to Love Your Enemies

Matthew 5:43–48

43 *You have heard that it was said, "Love your neighbor and hate your enemy."* 44 *But I tell you: Love your enemies and pray for those who persecute you,* 45 *that you may be sons of your Father in heaven. He causes his sun to rise on the evil and the good, and sends rain on the righteous and the unrighteous.* 46 *If you love those who love you, what reward will you get? Are not even the tax collectors doing that?* 47 *And if you greet only your brothers, what are you doing more than others? Do not even pagans do that?* 48 *Be perfect, therefore, as your heavenly Father is perfect.*

Revenge is the way of the world. In the week of writing this chapter, the BBC program, Kilroy, was on the subject of revenge. The host, Robert Kilroy Silk asked the question: "Is it possible to love our enemies?" Most of the participants thought it was neither possible nor right to do so. To the question, "Should we take revenge?" among the replies were the following:

"Most certainly."

"I cannot allow him to get away with it."

"You feel a lot better when you've done it."

"You get satisfaction in your heart if you hurt them as they hurt you."

"I'll shoot him so he doesn't do what he's done to me to someone else."

"Revenge can do you good."

"If you don't take revenge, you lose your self-respect."

Each time one of the participants described the actions they had taken to get revenge, there was a round of applause and cheers from the others.

For many their replies were understandable. One had suffered sexual abuse, another the loss of a limb through a medical error, another had a husband who had had an affair with her sister. In circumstances like these, how can we love our enemies? And why should we do so anyway?

We come now to what has been described as "the central and most famous section"[57] of the Sermon on the Mount. This is the first time that the word "love" has been mentioned. The Old Testament taught, "Love your neighbor" (Leviticus 19:18). Nowhere in the Old Testament does it say, "Hate your enemy." Again, Jesus was dealing with a scribal misinterpretation of the Old Testament. The command to "love your neighbor" was interpreted as being limited to other Jews and therefore it was permissible and indeed right to hate (or at least "love less"[58]) those outside Israel. Similar teaching is found in the Qumran community, which we know about from the Dead Sea Scrolls: "That they (members of the sect) may love all the sons of light, each according to his lot in God's design, and hate all the sons of darkness, each according to his guilt in God's vengeance."[59] There is no Old Testament warrant for such an attitude. Indeed, even in the Old Testament there are a number of passages suggesting the opposite (Exodus 23:4–5; Deuteronomy 22:1–4; Proverbs 25:21).

Yet no passage in the Old Testament goes as far as Jesus does here. Indeed, there is no parallel in Jewish literature to the "sweeping universality" [60] of the teaching of Jesus. We are to love our enemies, regardless of race, color, creed, or background; regardless of what harm they have done us and how much revenge seems to be justified.

This teaching was not purely hypothetical for the disciples. They had no doubt been insulted and derided, mocked for their humility and apparent weakness, and been unjustly accused of being dangerous revolutionaries. In due course they were to suffer far more serious forms of persecution; to be flogged, tortured, and many of them executed for their faith. Yet Jesus says to them, "Love your enemies." Understandably they must have been thinking, "What does this mean?" and, "Why should we?" Jesus anticipates these questions and gives the answers in the verses that follow.

WHAT DOES IT MEAN TO LOVE OUR ENEMIES?

Jesus says, "Pray for those who persecute you" (vs. 44) (or as it says in Luke's version, "those who abuse you"). The NIV footnote points out that some late manuscripts read, "Love your enemies, bless those who curse you, do good to those who hate you." This was probably not in the original of Matthew's Gospel, but it is certainly there in the teaching of Jesus (Luke 6:27–28).

First, we are to love our enemies *by our words*—"Bless those who curse you" (Luke 6:28). We are to reply to insults with compliments. It is usually possible to find something positive to say. The writer of Proverbs points out, "A gentle answer turns away wrath" (Proverbs 15:1). A gracious reply to a rude and aggressive comment can turn a potential enemy into a lifelong friend.

Secondly, we are to love our enemies *by our deeds*—"Do good to those who hate you" (Luke 6:27). This begins first and foremost with forgiveness, but it also involves positive action. "If your enemy is hungry, give him food to eat; if he is thirsty, give him water to drink" (Proverbs 25:21).

I once heard the evangelist Luis Palau speak of a young Lutheran minister in East Germany called Oubar Holmer. He had a wife and three children. When the Communists took over East Germany after the war and began to force people out of work, Holmer started to complain to the Communist authorities. This antagonism toward them made him very unpopular. His children were academically brilliant and wanted to go on to college after finishing high school, but the authorities hadn't forgotten Holmer's opposition to them during those early days. As a result, not one of his three children was ever able to get a university education. Years later the Communist regime fell in eastern Europe and Erich Honecker, the head of the Communist party, was ostracized. Nobody would touch him. They threw him out of his house. So Oubar Holmer called together his wife and three children, who were by then married, and said to them, "Nobody wants to receive Honecker. Do you think we should invite him to our home?" He said to his children, "Would you open up the bedroom that used to be yours and let Honecker sleep there?" His family said, "If God in Christ has forgiven us our sins, we will forgive Honecker for all the evil he has done to us, for the university education we never received and for the troubles we have had." And so Erich Honecker stayed with them for about nine months until their neighbors made it so hard for them that they had to let him go and he went over to Russia.

Thirdly, we are to love our enemies *by praying for them*—"Pray for those who persecute you" (vs. 44). As Bonhoeffer put it, "Through the medium of prayer we go to our enemy, stand by his side, and plead for him to God. . . . For if we pray for them, we are taking their distress and poverty, their guilt and perdition upon ourselves, and pleading to God for them."[61] Prayer is the acid test of whether or not we truly have love for someone. Coming into the light of God's presence reveals the true feelings in the depths of our hearts which words can sometimes cover over.

One of the most moving examples of this I have come across is the prayer of former Cypriot Bishop H. B. Dehqani-Tafti, after his son was murdered in cold blood:

> O God,
> We remember not only Bahram but also his murderers;
> Not because they killed him in the prime of his youth and made our hearts bleed and our tears flow;
> But because through their crime we now follow Thy footsteps more closely in the way of sacrifice.
> It makes obvious as never before our need to trust in God's love as shown in the Cross of Jesus and His resurrection;
> Love which makes us free from hate towards our persecutors;
> Love which teaches us how to prepare ourselves to face our own day of death.
> O God, Bahram's blood has multiplied the fruit of the Spirit in the soil of our souls;
> So when his murderers stand before Thee on the Day of Judgment
> Remember the fruit of the Spirit by which they have enriched our lives,
> And forgive.[62]

WHY SHOULD WE LOVE OUR ENEMIES LIKE THIS?

There are many good and practical reasons for loving our enemies. First, hate multiplies hate. It leads to a vicious circle of quarreling, unkindness, and misery. We all know families, relationships, firms, and organizations ripped apart by hate. The only way to break the vicious circle is with love.

Secondly, hate is self-destructive. Returning hate scars the soul and distorts the personality. One of the features of the Kilroy program I mentioned earlier on the topic of revenge was the anger and bitterness written across the faces of those who insisted on revenge. Hate wastes our time and energy. It eats away at us and eventually destroys us from the inside. We may feel we have "every right" to hate someone. But it is no good standing on our rights if it kills us. Canon Keith de Berry used to recite this little poem:

> This is the story of Jonathan Jay,
> Who died defending his right of way.
> He was right, dead right, as he went along,
> But now he's as dead as if he were wrong.

Thirdly, love is the way to transform an enemy into a friend. Abraham Lincoln had an arch-enemy named Edwin Stanton. Stanton hated Lincoln and used every ounce of his energy to degrade him in the public eye, even down to his physical appearance. When Lincoln was elected President, he was looking for someone to fill the vital post of Secretary of War. He chose Stanton, knowing all that he had said and done and in spite of the advice of those close to him, because he was the best man for the job. When Lincoln was assassinated, many men spoke laudable words about him. But the words of Stanton were the most moving. He used the immortal phrase, "He now belongs to the Ages," and referred to Lincoln as one of the greatest men that ever lived. The power of Lincoln's love had transformed Stanton from an enemy to a friend.

Yet it is none of these reasons that Jesus gives. He gives two quite different reasons. First, to love our enemies is to imitate our Father in heaven: "That you may be sons of your Father in heaven" (vs. 45).

God's love extends even to those who are hostile toward Him. "He causes his sun to rise on the evil and the good, and sends rain on the righteous and the unrighteous" (vs. 45). Sometimes it seems that the unrighteous flourish even more than the righteous.

The second reason Jesus gives is that it is love like this that marks us out from the world. "If you love those who love you, what reward will you get? Are not even the tax collectors doing that?" (vs. 46).

Even the hated tax collectors were capable of loving each other. As the Living Bible puts it, unbelievers are on the whole "friendly to friends," with the attitude: "You scratch my back and I'll scratch yours." But this love is usually limited to our own circle of friends and seldom extends to those who have done us harm. If that is our attitude as Christians, what are we doing "more than others" (v. 47)? The Greek word for "more than" means "that which is not usually encountered among men."[63] We are called to be different. We are called to what Bonhoeffer calls the "extraordinary . . . the hallmark of the Christian."[64]

There was one West Indian woman on the Kilroy program who had a radiant expression. When Robert Kilroy Silk asked her, "Should we forgive?" she replied, "Absolutely—my forgiving released me to get on with my life. You forgive and you get the healing which causes you to be a better person." She had been living with a man and expecting his child. Her partner went on holiday and met another woman. Shortly afterward, he came back one day and said, "I'm married." She said it took three weeks to sink in and then the rage came. She started to plot. She went into the kitchen and took out a hammer and put it in a carrier bag. "I wanted to hammer his head in," she said. "I wanted to scar him in a way that he would always be reminded when he looked in the mirror. He would think, 'This is because of what I did to Mary.' " Kilroy asked, "What stopped you?" She replied, "I became a Christian. I was told I had to forgive." She shone like a beacon of light on that program. She urged the others to forgive and help others in similar situations rather than harboring bitterness. One man said to her, "This world is not like the way you preach. There are not too many like you around." To which Kilroy replied and ended the program by saying, "Perhaps there ought to be more."

Jesus' lifestyle was completely consistent with His own teaching. He demonstrated His love in His own life and then, supremely, in His death. He was abused, beaten, tortured, and crucified. With infinite dignity, self-control, and love He held His peace, saying: "Father, forgive them, for they do not know what they are doing" (Luke 23:34). This is not a sign of weakness or a sign that He had lost His self-respect. It was proof of enormous strength and courage in the face of appalling cruelty and unjust suffering. Jesus calls us to follow Him and tells us that when we do so the world will sit up and listen.

Mehdi Dibaj was an Iranian Christian who had spent nine years in prison for his Christian faith, and was sentenced to be executed. While awaiting his fate, he wrote his final testament, addressing it to his jailers. He wrote:

> I . . . beg the honored members of the court present to listen with patience to my defense and with respect for the Name of the Lord.
>
> I am a Christian, a sinner who believes Jesus has died for my sins on the cross and who by His resurrection and victory over death, has made me righteous in the presence of the Holy God. . . .
>
> In response to this kindness, He has asked me to deny myself and be His fully surrendered follower, and not fear people even if they kill my body, but rather rely on the Creator of life who has crowned me with the crown of mercy and compassion, and who is the great protector of His beloved ones and their great reward. . . .
>
> The love of Jesus has filled all my being and I feel the warmth of His love in every part of my body. God, who is my glory and honor and protector, has put His seal of approval upon me through His unsparing blessings and miracles. . . .
>
> The God of Daniel, who protected His friends in the fiery furnace, has protected me for nine years in prison and all the bad happenings have turned out for our good and gain, so much so that I am filled to overflowing with joy and thankfulness. . . .
>
> During these nine years He has freed me from all my responsibilities so that under the protection of His blessed Name I would spend my time in prayer and study of His Word, with heart searching and brokenness, and grow in the knowledge of my Lord. I praise the Lord for this unique opportunity. "You gave me space in my confinement, my difficult hard-

ships brought healing and Your kindnesses revived me." Oh what great blessings God has in store for those who fear Him! . . .

I have committed my life into His hands. Life for me is an opportunity to serve Him, and death is a better opportunity to be with Christ. Therefore I am not only satisfied to be in prison for the honor of His Holy Name, but am ready to give my life for the sake of Jesus my Lord and enter His kingdom sooner. . . .

May the shadow of God's kindness and His hand of blessing and healing be upon you and remain for ever. Amen.

With respect, Your Christian prisoner, Mehdi Dibaj. [65]

Jesus concludes this passage, as well as this whole section of the Sermon on the Mount, with an all-embracing demand: "Be perfect, therefore, as your heavenly Father is perfect" (vs. 48). The section began with a demand for a righteousness that exceeded that of the scribes and Pharisees (vs. 20). In the last few chapters we have seen six examples of what this means in terms of anger, lust, marriage, integrity, what we do when wronged, and now in terms of loving our enemies. Jesus concludes with what appears to be an impossible demand. Clearly human beings cannot be perfect as God is perfect. The Greek word means "having attained the intended purpose, complete, full grown, mature, fully developed."

Jesus requires that His disciples do not settle for second best. We are not to be content with being good as far as anger is concerned, but bad at integrity; or good at love, but bad at lust. We are called to the highest possible standard in all these areas. We are called to a wholehearted devotion to imitating our Father in heaven. We are to be totally different from the world around us. In short, we are to follow the example of Jesus.

10
How to Give

Matthew 6:1–4

[1] Be careful not to do your "acts of righteousness" before men, to be seen by them. If you do, you will have no reward from your Father in heaven.
[2] So when you give to the needy, do not announce it with trumpets, as the hypocrites do in the synagogues and on the streets, to be honored by men. I tell you the truth, they have received their reward in full. [3] But when you give to the needy, do not let your left hand know what your right hand is doing, [4] so that your giving may be in secret. Then your Father, who sees what is done in secret, will reward you.

Why do Christians fall away? Why do some seem to start off the Christian life with such enthusiasm and then appear to give up?

In the autumn of 1992, Michael Plant, a popular American yachtsman, commenced a solo crossing of the North Atlantic Ocean from the United States to France. He was an expert, who had circumnavigated the globe alone more than once. The sailing community universally acknowledged Michael Plant as a yachtsman whose seafaring skills were without equal. His mid-sized sailing boat, the Coyote, was the epitome of modern sailing lore. He had the best expertise, experience, and equipment.

Eleven days into the voyage radio contact with Michael Plant was lost. When the Coyote's radio silence persisted for several days a search was launched. The Coyote was found, floating upside down, by the crew of a freighter 450 miles northwest of the Azores Islands.

Everyone in the sailing world must have been surprised that when the Coyote was found it was upside down in the water. Sailing boats will always right themselves, even if a wind or wave were momentarily to push it over on its side or even upside down. In order for a sailing boat to maintain a steady course, and in order not to capsize but to harness the tremendous power of the wind, there must be more weight below the waterline than there is above it. Any violation of this principle of weight distribution means disaster. When the Coyote was built, an 8,000-pound weight was bolted to the keel for this very reason. No one knows why or how, but the weight beneath the waterline broke away from the keel. The four-ton weight was simply missing. When that occurred, the boat's stability was compromised. The result was that a very capable, experienced, and much-admired man was lost at sea.[66]

In this section of the Sermon on the Mount, Jesus examines that part of our Christian life that is below the waterline. The same principle is true. There must be more weight below the waterline than there is above it. So what is the equivalent to the weight below the waterline? It is the part of our Christian life which no one else can see—our secret life with God.

At the beginning of the Sermon on the Mount (Matthew 5:1–16, my Chapters 1–2), Jesus spoke about what sort of people we should be as Christians. In the next section (Matthew 5:17–48, my Chapters 3–9), He spoke about how we should live out the Christian faith in the world. Now, in this section (Matthew 6:1–18, my Chapters 10–12), he speaks about our intimate relationship with our Father in heaven. It is the strength of this that will decide whether or not we will have a strong and healthy Christian faith.

The earlier part of the sermon was mainly concerned with our relationships with others, sometimes referred to as those on the "horizontal" level. We now move to the "vertical" relationship, our relationship with God. The Christian life involves both.

When Jesus was asked which was the greatest commandment of the law, He replied, " 'Love the Lord your God with all your heart and with all your soul and with all your mind.' This is the first and greatest commandment. And the second is like it: 'Love your neighbor as yourself' " (Matthew 22:37–39). Some argue that all that matters is loving other people, but Jesus said the first commandment was to love God. Others have said or at least acted as though all that mattered was loving God and that it did not really matter so much how we treated others.

Such people are often unconcerned about starvation, unemployment, and other social problems.

Jesus taught that both the vertical and the horizontal relationships are vital. We are to love God and our neighbors; the two are inseparable and intertwined. But in this section of the Sermon on the Mount, the emphasis shifts from our love for our neighbor to our love for God.

In one of the most challenging sections of the entire Bible, Jesus looks at the three pillars of contemporary Jewish piety: giving, praying, and fasting. Again He contrasts how His followers should act with the actions of the Pharisees and the pagans. The religious people—the Pharisees—He called "the hypocrites" (vss. 2, 5, 16) who liked everyone to see how religious they were. They were ostentatious about their faith. The irreligious—"the pagans" (vs. 7)—had no reality about their relationship with God. When they prayed there was a "mechanical formalism." [67] Followers of Jesus are to be unlike both of these.

As He looks at giving, praying, and fasting in turn, Jesus' teaching follows the same pattern. Each section starts with a command to be unlike the hypocrites (vss. 2, 5, 16), because He says in each case "I tell you the truth, they have received their reward in full." He teaches how the Christian should be (vss. 3, 7 ff., 17 ff.), because "Then your Father, who sees what is done in secret, will reward you" (vss. 4, 6,–7).

The section is introduced by a general command: "Be careful not to do your 'acts of righteousness' before men, to be seen by them. If you do, you will have no reward from your Father in heaven" (vs. 1). The rest of the section is a commentary on this verse. Although Jesus commanded us to let our "light shine before men, that they may see your good deeds and praise your Father in heaven" (Matt. 5:16), our motive for living out the Christian life should be the glory of God and not our own glory. The key distinction lies in the phrase "to be seen by them."

Our motive should not be that we may be seen. Our Christian activity might be seen, but it must never be done for the sake of being seen. As A. B. Bruce put it, we should "show when tempted to hide and hide when tempted to show." [68]

HOW NOT TO GIVE (VS. 2)

Jesus introduced the first example with the words, "So *when* you give" (vs. 2). Jesus assumed that His disciples would give. A devout Jew would give in two ways: by the tithe, a tenth of his income (compulsory), and secondly by giving alms (voluntary). "To give alms was beyond the letter of the Law" with "special merit attached." [69] In total, a devout Jew would give away at least one-sixth of his income.

Jesus puts giving first in the catalog of secret activities in our relationship with God. He speaks about it even before He speaks about prayer. To the Jews, giving was the most sacred of all religious duties.

In addition to expressing the importance of giving, the rabbis forbade ostentatious giving. It was not the teaching of the rabbis which Jesus denounced; it was the practice of the Pharisees which fell short of this teaching and was hypocritical (vs. 2). The Greek word for "hypocrite" was originally used for an actor in a play and came to mean "someone who is pretending to be something they are not." Jesus parodies the giving of the Pharisees as if, when they gave, they sent the trumpeters on ahead, blowing a fanfare to draw the crowds

so that the maximum number of people would see their generosity, and so they would be "honored by men" (vs. 2). As we would say, they were "blowing their own trumpets."

Jesus says that if we give in order to get "honor from men," then that is exactly what we will get and no more. He says, "I tell you the truth, have received their reward in full." If we give in order to receive honor from other people, we may be able to bask in the warmth of their gratitude and praise, but that is all we receive. To gain such a reward from others is to lose it from God. Martyn Lloyd-Jones, in his commentary on these verses, invites us to examine our lives in the light of Jesus' words and asks the question, "How much remains to come to you from God?" He adds, "It is a terrifying thought."[70]

HOW TO GIVE (VSS. 3–4)

Jesus says that when we give, not only should we not tell others, but we are not even to tell ourselves. He says, "Do not let your left hand know what your right hand is doing" (vs. 3).

Jesus uses this figurative language to express the need for total secrecy. Our giving is not to be self-conscious. To avoid the danger of self-righteousness, self-congratulation, and pride, we ourselves are scarcely to know that we have given. Otherwise, "altruism has been displaced by a distorted egotism."[71]

Our giving should be the result of an overflowing love and kindness of heart. It should be impossible for us not to give. It should be a joy and delight, for "God loves a cheerful giver" (2 Corinthians 9:7). Our hearts should be so full of thanks to God for all that He has given us that we cannot wait to give in response to His love.

"You gave that much?
jolly good. well done."

When we give with this attitude Jesus says, "Then your Father, who sees what is done in secret, will reward you" (vs. 4). Some manuscripts have the word "openly," suggesting a contrast between hidden giving and an open reward. But the word "openly" is not in the most reliable manuscripts. What Jesus is contrasting is not the method of reward, but the source of the reward and therefore its quality. He is contrasting the wonderful reward which comes from a heavenly Father with the relatively miserly reward of human approval.

Many find the concept of reward distasteful and inappropriate in a Christian context. Surely, they say, we should give without expecting any reward at all. Isn't the idea of a reward worldly and materialistic? However, we must be careful not to try to be more spiritual than Jesus. Jesus spoke a good deal about rewards. True, this teaching has often been misunderstood and misrepresented. Neither Jesus nor the other New Testament writers ever promised us material prosperity in this life, but nevertheless they did speak in terms of rewards.

C. S. Lewis drew a very helpful distinction between different types of reward. He wrote:

> We must not be troubled by unbelievers when they say that this promise of reward makes the Christian life a mercenary affair. There are different kinds of rewards. There is the reward which has no natural connection with the things you do to earn it and is quite foreign to the desires that ought to accompany those things. Money is not the natural reward of love; that is why we call a man mercenary if he marries a woman for the sake of her money. But marriage is the proper reward for a real lover, and he is not mercenary for desiring it. A general who fights well in order to get a peerage is mercenary; a general who fights for victory is not, victory being the proper reward of battle as marriage is the proper reward of love. The proper rewards are not simply tacked on to the activity for which they are given, but are the activity itself in consummation. [72]

What then are the rewards of giving? Paul sets some of them out in 2 Corinthians 9:6–15. First, giving is the best investment we can make: "Whoever sows sparingly will also reap sparingly, and whoever sows generously will also reap generously" (vs. 6). This is the principle of the harvest. Giving is planting seed. It is investing for the future. Whatever we give to the Lord He multiplies, whether it is our spiritual gifts or our material possessions and money. If we lay up for ourselves treasures here on earth, then moth and rust consume them. It is only treasures in heaven that are permanent. If we want treasure in heaven, we have to send it on in advance. What we hold onto we lose, but what we give we keep forever.

Secondly, we will know God's love, "for God loves a cheerful giver" (vs. 7). That is why Paul urges us to give "not reluctantly or under compulsion." Our giving should not be out of sorrow, nor should it be forced out of stern duty or necessity. Giving should be fun. Receiving presents is fun, but giving them is even more enjoyable. That is why John Wimber often encourages people, when making out checks, to "whistle while you write."

There are no rules about how much we should give, only that it should be a generous proportion of what we have. Oswald Sanders points out that Jacob the swindler gave a tenth. Zacchaeus the despised tax collector gave a half. The unnamed and penniless widow gave "all she had to live on" (Mark 12:44). The devout Jew gave at least a sixth of his income. Jesus does not discuss what percentage we should give away. If we accept this teaching of Jesus we will realize that even to argue about percentages is to miss the point. It is not a matter of, "How much must I give away?" but, "How much do I need to keep?"

The late R. G. LeTourneau, the Texan industrialist, described in his autobiography the key question in relation to the gift of giving. In it he said,

> "The question is not how much of my money I give to God, but rather how much of God's money I keep." He answered it in his life by turning 90% of the assets of the company over to his Christian foundation, and then he and his wife gave in cash 90% of the income that was realized from the share of the business that he kept. He and his wife never lacked.[73]

The important point that Paul makes is that "each man should give what he has decided in his heart to give" (2 Corinthians 9:7).

Thirdly, giving frees us from financial worry. "And God is able to make all grace abound to you, so that in all things at all times, having all that you need, you will abound in every good work" (2 Corinthians 9:8). Giving does not mean handing over financial responsibility to God, but it does mean handing over the burden and the worry of the responsibility. God is no one's debtor. John Bunyan wrote:

> There was a man,
> They called him mad,
> The more he gave,
> The more he had.

One Christian leader told me that whenever he had an overdraft which he needed to pay off, he gave some money away and the result was that the Lord gave him so much that he was able to pay off his overdraft!

Hudson Taylor, the founder of the China Inland Mission, who determined "to move man through God, by prayer alone," saw thousands converted through his ministry and is seen by many as having laid the foundations for the present revival in China. At the age of 27 he was preparing to go to China. He was working hard, was ministering on Sundays and was living a very frugal life. One Sunday, after he had had a bowl of gruel the night before, porridge in the morning and nothing for supper, he was asked to go and pray for a poor man and his wife who was dying. He had one dollar in his pocket. He saw their poverty and wanted to give. He said that if he had had four quarters he would have given two. When he saw the poverty of the mother and her five children he felt he would gladly have given her one quarter. He then told them about the love of their heavenly Father, but he felt a hypocrite that he was not prepared to give to these people and trust God without breaking his one dollar piece into quarters. At this point he would gladly have given three quarters and kept only one. Eventually he said, "Well, you asked me to pray, so let's pray." He began, "Our Father. . . ." He struggled through the prayer. The father of the family said, "If you can help us, for God's sake do." After a tremendous struggle, he gave the one-dollar coin. Joy flooded his heart. He sang all the way home and as he ate his gruel, he reminded the Lord that "he that giveth to the poor, lendeth to the Lord." He slept peacefully. The following morning, he was surprised to receive a letter—he had not been expecting anything. Inside he found a pair of gloves and four dollars. He had received a 400% return in 12 hours. This incident was a turning point, and he came back to it time and again because through it he had learned to trust God in little things. It helped him in the more serious trials of life.[74] Giving is a virtuous circle.

Fourthly, giving transforms our whole character. "He . . . will enlarge the harvest of your righteousness" (2 Corinthians 9:10). Giving pries our characters from the constricting grip of materialism which destroys so many lives. John Wesley said, "When I have any money I get rid of it as quickly as possible, lest it find a way into my heart."

Ebenezer Scrooge, the central character in Dickens's *A Christmas Carol*, was a mean old businessman.

> Oh! but he was a tight-fisted hand at the grindstone, Scrooge! A squeezing, wrenching, grasping, scraping, clutching, covetous old sinner! Hard and sharp as flint, from which no steel had ever struck out generous fire; secret, and self-contained, and solitary as an oyster. The cold within him froze his old features, nipped his pointed nose, shriveled his cheek, stiffened his gait; made his eyes red, his thin lips blue; and spoke out shrewdly in his grating voice. [75]

He underpaid his clerk, neglected his clerk's family, wouldn't help his clerk's crippled son, Tiny Tim, and he refused to give a penny of his money away to the poor. We see how money had become his god and he had lost his life and even his marriage because of it. When he is shown his past, present and future, he sees that by keeping his money he is destroying his soul. He also realizes that he has the power, by giving it away, to change other people's lives. He repents, he starts to give, he doubles his clerk's salary, sends him a turkey, gives a salary to the poor, and becomes a second father to Tiny Tim. Dickens captures the transformation in his character:

> He went to church, and walked about the streets, and watched the people hurrying to and fro, and patted children on the head, and questioned beggars, and looked down into the kitchens of houses, and up to the windows, and found that everything could yield him pleasure. He had never dreamed that any walk—that anything—could give him so much happiness. [76]

Fifthly, we have the joy of seeing others giving thanks and praise to God as a result of the gift. "Through us your generosity will result in thanksgiving to God. This service that you perform is not only supplying the needs of God's people but is also overflowing in many expressions of thanks to God. Because of the service by which you have proved yourselves, men will praise God. . . ." (2 Corinthians 9:11b–13a). We are like cups filled from a spring. Others drink from us and praise not the cup but the spring.

Sixthly, we have the joy and satisfaction of "supplying the needs of God's people" (2 Corinthians 9:12). We become part of the community of the church as we share in its needs: "Your generosity in sharing with them and with everyone else" (2 Corinthians 9:13b). We know the peace that comes from obeying God, "The obedience that accompanies your confession of the gospel of Christ" (2 Corinthians 9:13).

Seventhly, we will have the reward of knowing that we are doing what Jesus did (2 Corinthians 9:15). This is the supreme example of giving. Bill Gates, the founder and chairman of Microsoft, has a few billion dollars and is acquiring a few more. Napoleon conquered a few countries. Alexander the Great conquered the whole known world of his day. But all these are like children playing Monopoly compared to what Jesus owns. The entire universe with all its billions of stars belongs to Him. It was all created through Him. He was rich, yet for you and for me He became poor, so that we might become rich. We are now co-heirs with Him. We will inherit all that He has. In the meantime, He asks us to follow in His steps and give generously.

11
How to Pray

Matthew 6:5–15

[5] And when you pray, do not be like the hypocrites, for they love to pray standing in the synagogues and on the street corners to be seen by men. I tell you the truth, they have received their reward in full. [6] But when you pray, go into your room, close the door and pray to your Father, who is unseen. Then your Father, who sees what is done in secret, will reward you. [7] And when you pray, do not keep on babbling like pagans, for they think they will be heard because of their many words. [8] Do not be like them, for your Father knows what you need before you ask him.

[9] This, then, is how you should pray:

"Our Father in heaven,
hallowed be your name,
[10] your kingdom come,
your will be done
    on earth as it is in heaven.
[11] Give us today our daily bread.
[12] Forgive us our debts,
    as we also have forgiven our debtors.
[13] And lead us not into temptation,
but deliver us from the evil one."

[14] For if you forgive men when they sin against you, your heavenly Father will also forgive you. [15] But if you do not forgive men their sins, your Father will not forgive your sins.

The best way to learn to do something well is to learn from an expert. I have always been a big fan of cricket. I used to spend hours listening to *Test Match Special* and reading old Wisden cricketers' almanacs. I was never good enough to be on a team, but I practiced for hours. When it came to playing I was almost invariably out, and when I bowled, I was so wild that fielders nearby were in danger of being hit on the head. On the other hand, I can only sit and admire my sons as they play cricket. It is a joy to watch as they have both been coached by experts. If we want to learn how to pray, we need to receive instruction from the greatest expert of all—Jesus Christ.

Jesus taught His disciples how to pray and assumed they would do so, because three times He says, "When you pray" (vss. 5–7). The Jewish people prayed regularly. Twice a day they recited a prayer called the "Shema" (Hear, O Israel . . .), and three times a day the people prayed the "Tephillah," a complex series of blessings upon God's people. Jesus clearly expected His disciples to pray daily (vs. 11).

But how should they pray? In this passage Jesus lays down four invaluable guidelines.

SINCERITY (VS. 5)

He says, "When you pray, do not be like the hypocrites, for they love to pray standing in the synagogues and on the street corners to be seen by men. I tell you the truth, they have received their reward in full" (vs. 5).

Jesus is not criticizing public worship or corporate prayer—He is warning against doing so for the wrong motives, hoping that others will be impressed by our spirituality. If we go to a prayer meeting in order simply to be seen by other people, that is the only reward we will get. We are hypocrites because we are pretending to be spiritual when we are not. We are insincere. The right motive for prayer is a desire to encounter our Father in heaven.

SECRECY (VS. 6)

Jesus says, "When you pray, go into your room, close the door and pray to your Father, who is unseen. Then your Father, who sees what is done in secret, will reward you" (vs. 6).

Jesus encourages His followers to get alone with God in a secret place. No doubt part of the reason for this is that there are no distractions. In our household, the only time when there are no distractions is early in the morning, before the children get up and before the telephone starts ringing. Here, though, Jesus is thinking more of ostentation than distractions. To "go into your room" is a metaphorical way of denoting privacy and the absence of admirers.

The Greek word for "room" means "inner room" which was also a store room where treasures might be kept. It is here that "your Father, who sees what is done in secret, will reward you" (vs. 6). What we seek is what we get. If we seek the reward of the admiration of others, then that is all we will get. If we seek to encounter God, then that will be our reward. We will experience His love for us and be filled with love for others. He will make His presence known to us. "You will fill me with joy in your presence," writes the psalmist (Psalm 16:11).

We will be able to get rid of our guilt, our problems, and our burdens and find a peace which passes understanding. We will gain a new perspective on life as we begin to see things from God's perspective. We will hear His voice and receive His guidance for our lives. We will have the joy of seeing our prayers answered. We receive power for living as He fills us with His Spirit. In comparison to this and the countless other blessings that God gives us, the rewards of being seen by others pale into insignificance.

SIMPLICITY (VSS. 7–8)

Whereas the hypocrites pray from a wrong motive, Jesus said that the pagans pray in a wrong manner. "And when you pray, do not keep on babbling like pagans, for they think they will be heard because of their many words. Do not be like them, for your Father knows what you need before you ask him" (vss. 7–8).

The pagans did not pray to the one true God but to a whole panoply of gods. In order to be sure that they were addressing the right god by the right name, they addressed all the gods with all their various titles. What mattered, they thought, was the correct repetition rather than the worshiper's attitude and intention. Jesus denounced such formal invocation and magical incantations as "babbling."

Moreover, the pagans had a mathematical notion of prayer. They believed that the longer they prayed the more likely they were to be heard. Jesus said that it is not the length of prayer that counts but its sincerity; the quality rather than the quantity.

He was about to teach them a prayer with only 57 Greek words, which can be prayed in less than 30 seconds.

Jesus was not against repetition in prayer, but He was against *mindless* repetition.

"heal the cat
heal the cat
heal the cat
heal the cat
heal the cat
heal the cat"

Indeed He taught His disciples to be persistent in prayer, to go on asking, to go on seeking, to go on knocking. He taught them two parables to this effect. One went like this: suppose you get a surprise visit from a friend who has been abroad for some time. It is late at night and the fridge is completely empty, so you run over to see a friend, whom you know always has lots of food in his house. You ring the doorbell and find that he is already asleep. He wakes up and tells you to go away and come back in the morning. However, you persist and say, "I really need that food now." Because you insist, he gets the food for you (see Luke 11:5–8).

Secondly, in order to show His disciples that "they should always pray and not give up," He told them a story about a terrible old judge who was not remotely interested in justice. He was totally godless. A woman who had lost her husband was in a dispute with her neighbor and so she took legal action. The judge was not interested, but she kept coming back. Eventually the judge decided that it

127

was easier to give her justice than to have to put up with her coming to court the whole time (see Luke 18:1–8).

Jesus Himself in the Garden of Gethsemane repeated the same prayer three times. But neither the prayer of Jesus, nor that which He taught His disciples, was mindless repetition intended to impress by its length. Jesus cried out to His Father from the agony of His situation. Likewise, when we are weighed down, we cannot help but cry out constantly to God to answer our prayers.

Jesus points out that we do not pray like this in order to inform God of something He does not know about, "for your Father knows what you need before you ask him" (vs. 8).

Rather, God gives us the privilege of being involved in His plans. In that sense prayer is for our benefit, not for His.

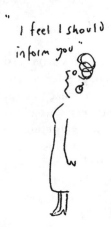

STRUCTURED (VSS. 9–16)

Jesus goes on to give His disciples a model for prayer. It is not intended to be the only model, but it is the most simple and yet the most refined. It is comprehensive and universal in that it covers in principle everything that we could ask of God. Essentially, it is supplication (asking). Adoration, praise, and thanksgiving are very important, but we are not to look down on asking as the lowest form of prayer. Supplication is at the very heart of the prayer which Jesus taught His disciples. Sadly, it has often been prayed mechanically, which is exactly what Jesus has just been teaching us not to do. However, many have found it to be the most wonderful structure for prayer.

Our Father in heaven. The prayer begins with a recollection of who we are approaching. Almost certainly, Jesus originally prayed and taught His disciples to pray in Aramaic. The word He used for Father was "Abba," a word which conveys intimacy like the English word "Daddy," but without the childish connotations. It is also quite extraordinary that Jesus tells us to go into a secret room, shut the door, and then pray, "Our Father . . ." and not, "My Father. . . ." Here is a clear sense of being part of God's family, praying with many others.

As we begin to pray it is crucial that we appreciate what we are doing. We are speaking to God. The realization of this fact transforms our prayers. We are not talking to ourselves or meditating. We are speaking to a person who is as real as we are, if not more so. Moreover, He is a loving Father with heavenly power. This realization should lift our hearts to praise, adoration, and thanksgiving as we begin to pray. I find this is the appropriate moment to thank God for all His blessings, such as health, family, friends, ministry, and answered prayers.

Hallowed be your name. The name of God means the revelation of who He is. Our first concern should be for God's name to be honored. According to the U.S. Center for World Missions, the Christian church is growing at a rate three times faster than the world population. However, in the United Kingdom this is not the case. God's name is seldom honored in the media or in schools. The supreme cry of our hearts should be to see His name honored.

At a personal level I find it helpful to pray through the day in my mind, asking that God's name would be honored in all the areas in which I am involved, such as meetings, work, relationships, and ministry.

Your kingdom come. Our country desperately needs Jesus. When we pray for His kingdom to come we are praying for His rule and reign to transform it, whether in the political arena, economics, social injustice, the rise in crime, or our schools.

Again, I also find it helpful to pray for His kingdom to come in the areas in which I am directly involved. This is a good heading under which to intercede for our friends, family, and colleagues.

In addition, it is a prayer for His return. The early Christians regularly prayed "Maranatha!"—"Come, Lord Jesus!" We long for His return, for that is when the kingdom will come fully on the earth. It is something to look forward to and pray for constantly. But it isn't simply in the future.

Your will be done. This is not a prayer of resignation, but a desire to know God's will and to see God's will done in our lives. God's will for us is "good, pleasing and perfect" (Romans 12:2). We need to know God's will for our lives, whether for the big issues like marriage and career, or the details of our lives as we go through each day.

Give us today our daily bread. This is not the place to start, but Jesus teaches us that our most basic material needs should be included in our prayers. Nothing is too small to pray about. It is good to go through the day in our prayers, asking God for what we need, whether it be housing, food, or driving in our cars.

Forgive us our debts as we also have forgiven our debtors. Jesus enlarges on this: "For if you forgive men when they sin against you, your heavenly Father will also forgive you. But if you do not forgive men their sins, your Father will not forgive your sins" (vss. 14–15). Jesus told the story about a foreign king who was owed the equivalent of $15 million by a civil servant. The man could not pay and so the king ordered that everything he had be sold, that bankruptcy proceedings be taken against him, and that his wife and children be sold into slavery. The man begged for mercy and asked for time to pay. The king, in an extraordinary act, forgave him the entire debt. The civil servant himself was owed $3,000 by another man. He grabbed this man and demanded instant payment. This man begged for mercy, but the civil servant took him to court and eventually the man was jailed for nonpayment of the debt. The king got to hear about this and was furious. He had the civil servant arrested and said to him, "You evil man. I let you off a debt of $15 million just because you asked me—shouldn't you have done the same to others?" He ordered the man to be sent to the torturers until he had paid the last penny. Jesus said, "This is how my heavenly Father will treat each of you unless you forgive your brother from your heart" (see Matthew 18:23–35). There is a connection between forgiving and receiving forgiveness. We do not earn forgiveness by forgiving others, but it is the evidence that we have received forgiveness. Daily we need to receive forgiveness and daily we need to forgive.

And lead us not into temptation, but deliver us from the evil one. The word used for temptation can mean either "temptation" or "testing." God does not tempt us with evil (James. 1:13). However, He is in charge of how much we are exposed to the temptations of the devil (see, for example, Job), and He does allow us to be tested. Here we are praying, in effect, "Grant that we will not fail the test." We are all tempted and we need God's protection and His power. This is a good place to pray that God would fill us with His Spirit and equip us for the day ahead.

As we have seen, Jesus promises that when we pray, God rewards us. One of these rewards is the joy of seeing our prayers answered. Late on a Sunday night in December 1987, I received a telephone call from a man who had been at our evening service. His name was James. He had been an actor, playing famous roles for many years. At one point in his life, he seemed to have everything: a beautiful wife, success, fame, and money. Then in December 1986, his wife, Anna, left him after three years of marriage. He had tried to forgive his

131

wife, but had not been able to. He felt he would not be able to forgive until he himself had experienced forgiveness. That day he prayed a prayer, repenting of his sins, thanking Jesus for dying for him and inviting the Holy Spirit to come and fill him. His life was transformed and he was able to forgive his wife. Into his heart came a longing for Anna to come back, but she would not. She had moved in with another man. She wanted a divorce and had begun proceedings.

James and all his new-found Christian friends began to pray for a reconciliation in their marriage. He tried to see her again, but she was not willing to meet him. I wrote, via her lawyer, and asked her whether she would be willing to come and see me. When she came I asked her to see James again for half an hour. Two days later she wrote and said she did not want to see James again.

James continued to pray and seek the Lord's guidance. He felt that if Anna wanted a divorce he should not stand in her way. He reached a point where he was more concerned that she should find Christ than that they should get back together again. He sent her and her new partner two tickets to go and hear Billy Graham in July, 1989. She sent them back. As it happens, Billy Graham decided to stay on for an extra night at Wembley stadium. James sent her two more tickets. By this stage the decree nisi (the first stage of the divorce) had come through. Anna rang James and said that her partner did not want to come, but she would like to go and hear Billy Graham. I think she felt safe to go with him as her decree nisi had come through. On the Saturday evening they went together to Wembley stadium.

The following morning I was preaching at St. Paul's, Onslow Square. While sitting in the front row, I turned around and saw James and Anna coming into the church together. I had never seen them together before. They came and sat down next to me. I was dying to find out whether Anna had gone forward to give her life to

Christ at the Billy Graham crusade. I did not like to ask the question directly, but I knew it had been raining the night before, so I asked, "Did you get wet?" She replied, "Yes, I got soaked out on the field."

After the service, they came to lunch. It turns out that she had gone forward in tears at the Billy Graham event. A counselor had approached her and asked whether she had come with someone. She said, "Yes." The counselor asked whether the person was a Christian. Again, she replied, "Yes." The counselor suggested she go and get the person. She said, "But it's my husband." The counselor said, "That's great!" Anna replied, "But you don't understand. I haven't seen him for two-and-a-half years!" At this point the counselor herself burst into tears.

As a result of giving her life to Christ, Anna left her adulterous relationship and returned to her husband James. They had to go to court to get the decree nisi set aside. The judge was delighted and the usher was in tears of joy. Now, six years later, they have two children and are lay pastors in the church.

On Monday, July 10, 1989, I wrote this in my prayer diary:

> Praise you, Lord, so much for yesterday—the best day that I can remember. Praise you, Lord, for your greatness and power and love. Thank You so much for Anna going to hear Billy Graham. Thank You that she went forward. Thank You that she stayed the night with James. Thank You that she came to St. Paul's. Thank You that she prayed the prayer. Thank You that she decided to go back to James. Thank You for her and James coming to lunch afterward. Thank You for the joy of seeing them together. Thank You that You are a God who answers prayer. Lord, I love You so much. I commit myself back to You to serve You with all my heart, all my life. "Is anything too hard for the Lord?"

12
How to Fast

Matthew 6:16–18

[16] When you fast, do not look somber as the hypocrites do, for they disfigure their faces to show men they are fasting. I tell you the truth, they have received their reward in full. [17] But when you fast, put oil on your head and wash your face, [18] so that it will not be obvious to men that you are fasting, but only to your Father, who is unseen; and your Father, who sees what is done in secret, will reward you.

When King George II was faced with the threat of invasion by the French in 1756, he called for a day of prayer and fasting. John Wesley recorded in his journal on Friday, February 6th: "The fast-day was a glorious day, such as London has scarcely seen since the Restoration. Every church in the city was more than full, and a solemn seriousness sat on every face. Surely God heareth the prayer, and there will yet be a lengthening of our tranquillity." In a footnote he wrote, "Humility was turned into national rejoicing for the threatened invasion by the French was averted."[77]

In the summer of 1876 a locust plague destroyed the crops of Minnesota farmers. In the spring of the following year they watched and waited to see whether such a pestilence would strike yet again. If it did, the farming future of thousands of families would be permanently wiped out. The constant unseasonal heat caused a vast army of locusts to hatch—a plague of such proportions as to threaten the entire north-west farm sector.

Acutely aware of the impending disaster, Governor J. S. Pillsbury proclaimed that April 26 would be a day of prayer and fasting to plead

134

with God to save them from calamity. The Governor urged everyone to take part. Across the state many people responded to their Governor's call. In gatherings large and small Minnesotans assembled to fast and pray.

After four days, with the locusts all hatched and ready to move,

a sudden climatic change at dusk flicked a blanket of frost across the entire area where the locusts waited for the dawn and take-off. Most were killed right where they crouched. Come summer, instead of scorched stubbled dirt, the wheat crop waved in golden glory as far as the eye could see. In the history of Minnesota, April 26, 1877 is recorded as a day when God wonderfully responded to the prayers and fasting of His people. [78]

In this section, Jesus moves from giving and praying to the third of the secret disciplines—fasting. In the Bible, fasting generally means going without all food for a specific period of time for spiritual reasons. We may distinguish it from a hunger strike, where abstinence from food is for political gain or to attract attention to a cause. It is also different from dieting, which stresses cutting out food for physical rather than spiritual reasons.

In the Old Testament there were certain annual fasts, such as on the Day of Atonement. In addition, there were occasional fasts, which were sometimes individual and sometimes corporate. Jesus Himself is recorded as fasting during His time in the wilderness (Matthew 4:2). It is clear from these verses that Jesus assumed that His disciples would fast. He did not say, "You must fast," which is legalistic. Nor did He say, "If you fast . . ." which is optional. Rather, He said to them, "When you fast . . ." (vs. 16). They did not need to be told to fast; they only needed instruction on how to do it properly. Once, when Jesus was asked why His disciples did not fast, He did not repudiate fasting in itself, but declared it to be inappropriate for His disciples as long as He was with them (see Matthew 9:14–15; Mark 2:18–20; Luke 5:33–34).

Later, when He was no longer with them, it would be right and proper for them to fast, as we see in the book of Acts. The leaders of the church fasted when choosing missionaries (Acts 13:2–3) and elders (Acts 14:23). Paul twice refers to fasting: once as a form of involuntary hunger (2 Corinthians. 11:27; 6:5) and on the other occasion as a form of voluntary self-discipline (1 Corinthians 9:27).

According to Epiphanius, Bishop of Salamis, fasting twice a week was the regular practice of all Christians in the fourth century. The Reformers, such as Luther, Calvin, Knox, and Latimer, all practiced prayer with fasting and claimed an increased effectiveness resulting in their ministries. John Wesley said that "some have exalted religious fasting beyond all Scripture and reason; and others have utterly disregarded it." [79] He did not wish a person to be ordained unless they agreed to fast at least twice a week until 4:00 P.M.

Jonathan Edwards, the revivalist and theologian, regarded fasting as the appropriate response when he was not seeing a spiritual breakthrough. He would fast and pray continuously for three days and nights.

> Over and over again he was heard praying, "Give me New England. Give me New England." When he finally arose from his knees and made his way into the pulpit, the people gazed at him as if they could almost see the face of God. When he began to speak, immediately conviction fell upon his audience. . . . He was extraordinarily empowered by the Spirit and it showed in the visible results of his evangelistic ministry. [80]

Paul Yonggi Cho, pastor of the world's largest church, in Korea, has seen astonishing growth in response to prayer. He writes: "We have seen that fasting and prayer causes one to become much more spiritually sensitive to our Lord, causing more power in one's life to combat the forces of Satan." [81]

WHY SHOULD WE FAST?

Once again, as with giving and praying, Jesus promises that those who fast in the right way will receive a reward from God. He says, "Your Father, who sees what is done in secret, will reward you" (vs. 18). God chiefly rewards those who fast with answered prayer and there are a number of reasons given in the Bible for fasting in connection with prayer.

First, fasting is often a way to reinforce prayer when asking God for a particular blessing. When Ezra was carrying a large consignment of gold and silver to the Temple in Jerusalem along a route infested with bandits, he records, "I proclaimed a fast, so that we might humble ourselves before our God and ask him for a safe journey for us and our children. . . . So we fasted and petitioned our God about this, and he answered our prayer" (Ezra 8:21, 23).

When the Benjaminites committed a terrible crime, the other tribes decided to go up against them. They did so, and were twice heavily defeated, even though they had prayed and wept before the Lord. However, the third time they fasted as well and God gave the other tribes overwhelming victory (Judges 20).

People who pray with fasting are giving notice that they are really in earnest: they do not intend to take "no" for an answer. They are showing earnestness in a divinely appointed way in order to be "heard on high." As Andrew Murray puts it, "Fasting helps to express, to deepen, and to confirm the resolution that we are ready to sacrifice anything, to sacrifice ourselves, to attain what we seek for the kingdom of God."[82]

Fasting like this can even cause God to "change His mind." When the prophet Jonah declared, on the instructions of the Lord, that Nineveh was about to be destroyed, "The Ninevites believed God. They declared a fast, and all of them, from the greatest to the least, put on sackcloth. . . . When God saw what they did and how they turned from their evil ways, he had compassion and did not bring upon them the destruction he had threatened" (Jonah 3:5, 10).[83]

Once, when the disciples asked why they couldn't drive out a certain demon, Jesus replied, "This kind can come out only by prayer." Many early and reliable Greek manuscripts read, ". . . by prayer *and fasting.*" Since Jesus cast the demon out with a mere word, He must be referring to activity which occurred before the occasion arose. He seems to be suggesting that the disciples had not spent enough time in prayer and that their spiritual strength was weak. Therefore, the "fasting" that is mentioned in many ancient manuscripts fits the pattern of an activity that increases one's spiritual strength and power. [84]

Still today, special enterprises require prayer which may include fasting. When Waymon Rogers, pastor of Christian Life Center in Louisville, Kentucky, and his congregation prayed constantly, their numbers grew from 200 to 2,000. However, when 200 of his people began to fast once a week, God's power increased dramatically. He reported:

> A woman with cancer was healed. God delivered people from demon possession. Many people were healed by the miraculous power of God. For four and a half months we had a revival where 10,000 people came each week to our church. They argued over who was going to get the front seats. People were saved and healed, and 4,600 people gave their hearts to God in that time. This was after the church had fasted and prayed for two years. The only problem we had was traffic jams. . . . Encourage your people to fast and pray! [85]

Secondly, fasting is a sign of repentance and humility before God. As the psalmist wrote, "I . . . humbled myself with fasting" (Psalm 35:13). God says to the people who have sinned against Him, "Even now . . . return to me with all your heart, with fasting and weeping and mourning" (Joel 2:12). Sometimes, fasting symbolized mourning and repentance over personal sin, as in the case of David when he had committed adultery with Bathsheba (2 Samuel 12:16–23).

Repentance means turning away from sin. Sometimes a particular sin begins to get a grip on our lives. The power of sin was broken on the cross, so sometimes a fast combined with prayer helps actualize what Jesus has achieved for us in our own lives.

At other times it was in connection with national sin. One person could confess and fast on behalf of the nation, as Daniel did over Israel's sin. He "turned to the Lord God and pleaded with him in prayer and petition, in fasting, and in sackcloth and ashes" (Daniel 9:3). He prayed to the Lord and confessed: "We have sinned and done wrong . . ." (Daniel 9:4 ff).

However, sometimes it was the whole nation which fasted and prayed. On one occasion Samuel assembled the people to pray at Mizpah: "On that day they fasted and there they confessed, 'We have sinned against the LORD' " (1 Samuel 7:6). Also, in the time of Ezra and Nehemiah, "The Israelites gathered together, fasting . . . confessed their sins and the wickedness of their fathers" (Nehemiah 9:1–2). God responded to their prayer and soon they were "rejoicing because God had given them great joy. The women and children also rejoiced. The sound of rejoicing in Jerusalem could be heard far away" (Nehemiah 12:43).

Thirdly, fasting is a way of seeking the Lord's guidance. Moses fasted 40 days and nights and was "with the Lord" before he recorded the Ten Commandments (Exodus 34:28; Deuteronomy 9:9). When Jehoshaphat saw that a large army of Moabites and others was coming to make war on Judah, he "resolved to inquire of the LORD, and he proclaimed a fast for all Judah. The people of Judah came together to seek help from the LORD; indeed, they came from every town in Judah to seek him" (2 Chronicles 20:3–4). When the church at Antioch was "worshiping the Lord and fasting, the Holy Spirit said, 'Set apart for me Barnabas and Saul for the work to which I have called them' " (Acts 13:2). Fasting also appears to have been a routine part of seeking the Lord's guidance with regard to appointing church leaders. On Paul's first missionary journey, he and Barnabas, as they traveled back through the churches they had planted, "appointed elders for them in each church . . . with prayer and fasting" (Acts 14:23).

Pastor Hsi (1830–1896) was one of China's greatest preachers. He had been an opium addict until he was dramatically converted at the age of 49. He opened rehabilitation centers, called Refuges, where opium addicts could, through the power of Christ, be delivered from their drug addiction. He was faced with a serious crisis in the early days of the opium Refuge work when the supply of foreign medicines failed. These were vital for the treatment of the patients. In this desperate situation the thought came to him that maybe God would use his knowledge of native drugs to create a medicine to take the place of the foreign supply. He sought the Lord with prayer and fasting, asking Him to reveal the proper ingredients. Mrs. Howard Taylor then records the sequel: "Very simply, it all came to him just how those pills were to be made. The drugs were at hand in his store, and, still fasting, he took the prescription, compounded the medicine, and hastened back to the Refuge." [86] It proved a success and entirely changed the aspect of opium refuge work.

In less dramatic ways, many people have found that in seeking the Lord's guidance about a major decision, it is helpful to combine prayer with fasting. I recently heard Sandy Millar, the vicar of Holy Trinity Brompton, say that before making two of the most important decisions in his life, the first regarding his marriage, the second about his calling to full-time ministry, on each occasion he set aside a weekend to fast and pray. It enables us to concentrate solely on one thing, and to give ourselves to praying.

Fourthly, fasting is a form of self-discipline. The apostle Paul uses the analogy of an athlete training for a race: "Everyone who competes in the games goes into strict training. They do it to get a crown that will not last; but we do it to get a crown that will last forever" (1 Corinthians. 9:25). His aim is that rather than being a slave to the passions of the body, the reverse should be true: his desire is to make his body a slave which serves him (1 Corinthians 9:24–27). Fasting helps to lessen the hold of material things upon us. It is easy to become self-indulgent and soft, doing nothing to deny ourselves. Fasting preserves us from becoming slaves to habits and it helps us to learn self-control. Overindulgence leads to our appetites being blunted and our palate dulled. Fasting helps us appreciate things all the more. One of the sins we hardly ever talk about is gluttony, or overindulgence. We all have more than enough, and it is good for us to exercise self-control and go without. It reestablishes our priorities.

William Bramwell, the early Wesleyan preacher, wrote to a friend in Liverpool in 1809: "The reason why the Methodists in general do not live in this salvation is, there is too much sleep, too much meat and drink, too little fasting and self-denial, too much conversation with the world, too much preaching and hearing, and too little self-examination and prayer." [87]

We can also be imaginative in fasting. It might not be food that has the biggest hold on us; perhaps it is books, CDs, pictures, or clothes. One young woman in our congregation went on a clothes "fast" for a year. She wanted to break the hold of the habit of buying clothes. For the first two weeks she found it very difficult, but after that she found the desire was broken. It also saved her a great deal of money!

Fifthly, one of the reasons for fasting is to share what we have with the undernourished. Isaiah 58 is one of the classic chapters on fasting in the Bible. God says that fasting in itself is not enough— it must be for the right motives.

> Is not this the kind of fasting I have chosen: to loose the chains of injustice and untie the cords of the yoke, to set the oppressed free and break every yoke? Is it not to share your food with the hungry and to provide the poor wanderer with shelter—when you see the naked, to clothe him, and not to turn away from your own flesh and blood? (Isaiah 58:6–7).

If we eat less, there should, at least in theory, be more to give away to the hungry. Further, we get a glimpse of what it is like to be hungry, to feel uncomfortable, and to have our sleep interrupted by hunger pangs. This should increase our compassion for the poor and the hungry and make us more aware of the need to "spend yourselves in behalf of the hungry and satisfy the needs of the oppressed" (Isaiah 58:10).

WHY NOT?

It is probably true that most Christians today do not fast—certainly in the West. It may be that they have never even thought about it. However, some have considered the matter and reject the practice of fasting. There are three main objections.

The first is a theological objection. When John's disciples came to Jesus they asked Him, " 'How is it that we and the Pharisees fast, but your disciples do not fast?' Jesus answered, 'How can the guests of the bridegroom mourn while he is with them? The time will come when the bridegroom will be taken from them; then they will fast' " (Matthew 9:14–15; see also Mark 2:18–20). Some have argued that the time when the bridegroom is taken away refers to the period between the cross and Resurrection. This is the period when Jesus was no longer with them. After the Resurrection He was with them again and after the Day of Pentecost He was with them by His Spirit. This is an attractive argument, but it will not bear examination and it is clearly not how the apostles understood Jesus. It was not until after His ascension that we read of them fasting (Acts 13:2–3). Surely the period Jesus was referring to was between His first coming and His second coming. The Church is still waiting for the midnight cry, "Here's the bridegroom! Come out to meet him!" (Matthew 25:6). During the present church age He has been "taken" away from us until the day He returns. "It is this age of the Church to which our Master referred when He said, '*Then* they will fast.' The time is *now*!"[88]

142

The second is a historical objection and a reaction to excessive asceticism. Fasting developed a bad reputation as a result of practices in the Middle Ages. With the decline of the inward practice of the Christian faith there was a tendency to stress outward devotion. Fasting was subjected to the most rigid regulation and was practiced with extreme self-mortification. The ascetic, "one who practices severe self-discipline," would renounce all physical comforts and normal social intercourse. Excessive asceticism could even involve self-inflicted harm and bodily torture, such as wearing a hair-shirt or a spiked girdle. Such practices are a result of three wrong attitudes: seeing God as a "hard man"; believing that salvation can be achieved by works; and considering the human body to be inherently evil.

As a reaction to this some have swung to the opposite extreme and fasting has been replaced by selfish ease and comfortable affluence.

It has often been pointed out that the opposite of abuse is not disuse but right use.

The third objection is a practical one. Some argue that fasting is unhealthy. It is true that it is not appropriate for all people to fast, and for some, there are good medical reasons for not fasting. Fasting is not sensible for those who are pregnant or breast-feeding; nor is it wise for a diabetic or someone who has a member of the family who is a diabetic. Those who are convalescing from surgery or illness or taking medication would also be ill-advised to fast, as would those who are stressed, depressed, or grieving from a recent loss. Certainly it would be most unwise for those liable to eating disorders.

Having said all that, it is not in itself unhealthy to fast. Indeed, an argument can be made that for most people it is a positive benefit to our health. With very little work for the intestinal tract to do, the body can use all its energy to break down tissue and eliminate toxins from the body. We are polluted by all the junk we put into our bodies. Food is full of toxic substances such as artificial colorings, preservatives, and taste enhancers. Fasting detoxifies the system, cleansing, healing, and resting vital organs such as the kidneys and the liver—it is like giving the body a good spring cleaning.

HOW SHOULD WE FAST?

Jesus says that there is a wrong way and a right way to fast. The blessings of fasting are not automatic, even in the Old Testament (Isaiah 58:2–12; Jeremiah 14:11–12; Zechariah 7). First, our fasting must not be ostentatious, like "the hypocrites."

Jesus ridicules the hypocrisy of going around gloomy-faced. The word for "disfigure" literally means "to make invisible." It is a play on the phrase "to be seen" and means "to make unrecognizable," either by covering the head or by smearing it with ash or dirt. In contrast, the right approach is to look normal, clean, and happy.

In practice, it is wise to learn to walk before we run. It is sensible to start with short fasts, perhaps missing a meal or two. Later on, we might progress to a three-day fast. Some have found it helpful to fast for up to a week. Occasionally, people have felt called to fast for even longer. Personally, I think such occasions are very rare. It is hard to carry out a job when fasting for a long period. There is a danger of simply becoming irritable and failing to function in the way that we should.

Before beginning a fast it is wise to prepare. Many advise eating a little less during the days beforehand and eating fresh fruit as the last meal before the fast. During the fast it is important to drink at least 10 glasses of water a day and to get plenty of rest. When ending a fast we need to be careful not to eat too much, as the stomach will have shrunk and will not be able to cope with a large meal.

Secondly, we are not to fast with a legalistic attitude. The bi-weekly fasts had become a recognized institution among pious Jews. They fasted on Mondays and Thursdays. These were market days and there was therefore a bigger audience. It is very easy for us also to slip back into legalism. We can see this from the commentary on this part of Jesus' teaching in paragraph 8 of the *Didache* ("The Teaching of the Lord to the Gentiles, through the Twelve Apostles"), usually dated around A.D. 100: "Do not keep the same fast-days as the hypocrites. Mondays and Thursdays are their days for fasting, so yours should be Wednesdays and Fridays." This shows how easy it was then, as now, to miss the point of Jesus' teaching.

Rather than fasting for legalistic reasons we should fast out of love for God. It is an element of our relationship with Him and we should fast when we sense His Spirit asking us to do so. Our fasting should always center on God. God questioned the people in Zechariah's day: "When you fasted and mourned . . . was it really for me that you fasted?" (Zechariah 7:5). John Wesley declared, "First, let it be done unto the Lord with our eyes singly fixed on Him. Let our attention herein be this and this alone, to glorify our Father which is in heaven. . . ."[89]

CONCLUSION

Omar Cabrera is one of the leaders at the center of the revival in Argentina. He started with a group of 12 people who fasted and prayed every week from Friday night to Sunday night, asking the Lord to move by His Holy Spirit. A girl who had a problem with her heart which the doctors had given up hope on, was healed by the Lord. Her father, a famous surgeon, spoke publicly about what had happened.

One woman worked as a maid. Her employer wanted to know where she was going and she came to the church as well. She had been involved in politics, but when the Lord touched her heart she left politics to work in the church.

After one year the group had grown from 12 to 120. They rented an Anglican chapel and began praying for a church of 2,000. Every Wednesday they studied Mark's gospel and underlined the words "great," "multitude," and "many." For nine months, they read, prayed, and fasted, and people began to come in large numbers.

Omar Cabrera found himself preaching every night and, at one stage, he preached 540 nights in a row. Sometimes 9–15,000 people came to the meetings and they saw great blessing. He would go aside for two to three days to pray and fast. In one year the church grew 1,000%, and by 1991 it had 90,000 members. He was serious about God. He prayed and he fasted, and God rewarded him.

13
How to Handle Money

Matthew 6:19–24

19 Do not store up for yourselves treasures on earth, where moth and rust destroy, and where thieves break in and steal. 20 But store up for yourselves treasures in heaven, where moth and rust do not destroy, and where thieves do not break in and steal. 21 For where your treasure is, there your heart will be also.

22 The eye is the lamp of the body. If your eyes are good, your whole body will be full of light. 23 But if your eyes are bad, your whole body will be full of darkness. If then the light within you is darkness, how great is that darkness!

24 No one can serve two masters. Either he will hate the one and love the other, or he will be devoted to the one and despise the other. You cannot serve both God and Money.

If we grasp Jesus' teaching in this section of the Sermon on the Mount, it will transform our lives. It will affect our security, our vision and ultimately our relationship with God. Yet few people seem to have caught hold of what Jesus is saying. A recent article in

The Independent on contemporary culture reports that teenagers nowadays say that they want money, and lots of it: "Top of everyone's priority list for a job is money. These teenagers are realists and unashamed materialists. They see their success as solely dependent on their own efforts. Status, power and happiness reside in acquiring wealth." [90] Whatever else we may say about the state lotteries, it reveals our obsession with acquiring wealth. Money, as well as sex, dominates much of our advertising.

Most of us have to deal with money every day, but we prefer not to talk about it in church. Jesus talked about it a great deal, however, and in this passage He puts before us a blunt choice between two options. In doing so, He echoes Elijah in the Old Testament, who asked the people: "How long will you waver between two opinions? If the LORD is God, follow him; but if Baal is God, follow him" (1 Kings 18:21). There is a stark choice to be made, and Jesus puts the choice in three different ways.

WHERE IS OUR SECURITY? (VSS. 19–21)

Jesus identifies two different places where we can store up treasure, and calls us to an undivided heart. Because our hearts will follow our treasure, He commands us not to store up treasure on earth, but in heaven. Treasure includes not only money, but possessions, clothes, homes, power, position, status, and possibly even intelligence, fame, popularity, athleticism, and good looks. These things do not ultimately satisfy because they do not last. "Moth" and "rust" destroy, and thieves break in and steal. Catherine Deneuve, once regarded as "the most beautiful woman in the world," was interviewed at the age of 45. She spoke about her fears of growing old: "It worries me, and it bores me. It is very painful to look in the mirror every day and watch yourself aging." Her treasure was decaying.

What does Jesus mean when He says that we are not to store up treasure on earth? His teaching has often been misunderstood and misinterpreted. First, He does not mean that all Christians are required to give away all that they have. In only one recorded case did He tell someone to give everything away (Mark 10:21). It seems that Joseph of Arimathea continued to be wealthy (Matthew 27:57) after he had become a disciple of Jesus, and the same is likely to be true of Nicodemus. During his ministry, Jesus was supported by wealthy women (Luke 8:1–3).

Secondly, it does not mean that it is wrong to invest or to make money. The parable of the talents speaks approvingly about making money. Some, it would seem, are called to make money, perhaps even large amounts of money, for the glory of God and for the purposes of His use in His kingdom. Some may be called to positions of power, wealth, and influence.

Thirdly, it is not wrong to save. The New Testament encourages us to provide for our relatives and especially for our own immediate family. Indeed, we have a duty to do so. Anyone who does not do so "is worse than an unbeliever" (1 Timothy 5:8). Jesus derided those who excused the fact that they were not looking after their own parents financially on the basis that they had set aside for God the money they would have used to look after them (Mark 7:9–12).

Saving enables us to provide for the needs of others.

Fourthly, it is not wrong to enjoy the good things of life. God has provided us with all things richly to enjoy (1 Timothy 6:17). Jesus ate with the rich and privileged (Luke 11:37), and went to a lavish wedding (John 2:1–11) and helped to make it even more lavish. He was even wrongly accused of being a glutton and a drunkard (Matthew 11:19). Wealth, at least in the Old Testament, was often seen as a sign of God's blessing; God blessed Abraham with cattle, silver, and gold, and Solomon's wealth was seen as evidence of God's favor. Under the New Covenant, God's blessing is not material but spiritual, but material things can still be gratefully enjoyed as undeserved gifts from God.

Jesus is concerned not so much with our wealth, but with our hearts and affections; that is, what we think about when our minds are in "neutral." He is concerned not so much with money as the love of money, which the apostle Paul describes as "a root of all kinds of evil" (1 Timothy 6:10). Jesus forbids the selfish accumulation of money and egocentric covetousness. In other words, He condemns materialism and the unhealthy obsession with and reliance on possessions. But He does so without despising material things in themselves.

Jesus explains this teaching in two ways. First, the very things which promise security lead to perpetual insecurity. I once heard Victor Matthew, who was brought up in the 1930s' depression, interviewed on the *Midweek* radio program. He said that he had felt the need for security, and had consequently made lots of money. When asked what effect this had had on his life, he replied: "For the first six weeks I woke up feeling secure. Then I started to worry about how I was going to hang on to all the money I had made." He concluded by saying that he had never found security. George Harrison, despite all the money he had made as one of the Beatles, said, "For every hundred dollars you earn you get a hundred dollars' worth of problems." As Seneca put it centuries before, "Money has never yet made anyone rich."

Secondly, materialism leads us away from God. Jesus says, "For where your treasure is, there your heart will be also" (vs. 21). As John Stott puts it, materialism "tethers our hearts to the earth."[91] For these reasons, Jesus says that it is a bad investment.

Instead of investing in storing up treasures on earth we should invest in storing up treasures in heaven. This is not describing a way of earning our salvation, but speaks of investing in the kingdom of heaven—God's rule and reign on the earth. Investing in His kingdom will primarily mean putting our time, energy, and money into people. It will mean, among other things, investing in preaching the Gospel, healing the sick, caring for the weak and lonely, and ministering to the poor. It will also include giving to other Christians to help their work. In A.D. 250, during the days of the Decian persecution in Rome, the Roman prefect burst into a church service and demanded, "Show me your treasures." They had come to take away everything of value. A deacon of the church called Lorencius showed him to an adjoining room, threw open the door and replied, "These are the treasures of our church." Inside was a group of widows, orphans, sick people, and paupers, all being cared for by members of the church.

Why should we invest in storing up for ourselves "treasures in heaven"? Again, Jesus gives us two reasons. First, this investment is totally secure and will last forever—"where moth and rust do not destroy, and where thieves do not break in and steal" (vs. 20). It is a good bargain to exchange the transitory for the eternal. God has given us an inheritance that can never "perish, spoil or fade" and that is "kept in heaven" for us (1 Peter 1:4). What we can see is temporary, "but what is unseen is eternal" (2 Corinthians 4:18). Paul wrote: "For I am convinced that neither death nor life, neither angels nor demons, neither the present nor the future, nor any powers, neither height nor depth, nor anything else in all creation, will be able to separate us from the love of God that is in Christ Jesus our Lord" (Romans 8:38-39).

Secondly, Jesus says that our hearts will follow our treasure (vs. 21). Giving is one of the secret disciplines Jesus spoke about in Matthew 6:1-4. As we give generously to the kingdom of God our hearts will follow our money. For example, people who give to the church are usually the ones who are most committed. It is not just that commitment leads to giving—although it does—but Jesus says that generous giving leads to commitment. Once we start investing in the kingdom of God we will become a great deal more interested in and committed to it. In these verses Jesus calls us to an undivided heart, and to committed action set on Jesus and His kingdom.

WHAT IS OUR AMBITION IN LIFE? (VSS. 22–23)

Jesus sets before us two goals in life and calls us to be single-minded. "The eye is the lamp of the body. If your eyes are good, your whole body will be full of light. But if your eyes are bad, your whole body will be full of darkness. If then the light within you is darkness, how great is that darkness!" (vss. 22–23). Jesus is using here the analogy of physical eyes. If our eyes are working properly we will have light inside. If our eyes are bad and we are blind, we have darkness. Sheila Hocken, who had been blind since infancy, had her sight restored at the age of 29 by an amazing and complex operation which was the result of months of intensive research. She wrote of the moment when the bandages were removed:

> I was suddenly hit, physically struck by the brilliance, like an immense electric shock into my brain. It flooded my whole being with a shock wave, this utterly unimaginable brightness. There was the white of a nurse's dress in front of me, a dazzling white I could hardly bear to take in, and behind her a vivid blue sky. It was fantastic. I felt that the whole of creation had been laid on for my personal benefit. [92]

At the spiritual level, it is true that the eyes are the windows of the soul, and so it matters a great deal where we set our spiritual sights—whether they are set on God or on materialism. What do we spend our time thinking about? What are we planning? What do we dream about? Where does our effort go? It is the eye that looks straight ahead, and we then move toward the object on which our gaze is fixed. When mowing the lawn, the way to mow in straight lines is to fix our eyes on an object at the other end of the yard. So it is in the spiritual realm: our hearts will follow our eyes. That is why the writer of Hebrews encourages us to "fix our eyes on Jesus" (Hebrews 12:2).

Those whose eyes are fixed on Jesus will have their bodies full of the light of the Spirit. A little boy was asked to define a "saint." At first he could not think of an appropriate definition, but then he thought of all the saints represented on stained-glass windows. He observed that "a saint is someone through whom the light shines." Sometimes this has an almost physical manifestation. On one occasion Jesus' face is described as shining "like the sun" (Matthew 17:2). There are some people who have "shining faces" and seem to radiate the light and love of God. They light up a room whenever they enter it.

One such is Jackie Pullinger, who has worked in Hong Kong for the last 28 years among drug addicts, the poor, and the homeless. She says that God gave her "resurrection eyes"; that is, eyes that see the living Christ. Like Paul, she is looking beyond this life to the time when she too will be raised with Christ. Her gaze is toward a distant city. She says, "Only Jesus opens eyes. . . . But all who believe in the Resurrection of the dead know their destination is a place of comfort, a better country, a heavenly city." [93]

On the other hand, Jesus warns us that if our eyes are bad our whole bodies will be full of great darkness (vs. 23). The word for "bad" literally means "evil." An evil eye is fixed not on Jesus but on selfish gain and materialism. It is set on obtaining more for ourselves. This eye is full of lust, greed, avarice, and resentment. Such an eye inevitably harbors jealousy, which Shakespeare described as "the green-ey'd monster which doth mock the meat it feeds on." [94] Once again there is often a physical manifestation—a darkness in people's eyes which reflects the darkness in their souls.

We are called to be single-minded, to set our thoughts and our sights on Jesus and His kingdom. We should seek a vision for our lives, whether it be raising up children for Christ, or serving God as a nurse, gardener, banker, lawyer, or farmer. It will also be a generous vision that does not seek gain for ourselves, but rather aims to serve Christ and others.

WHOM DO WE SERVE? (VS. 24)

In this verse, Jesus puts before us two gods and calls us to a surrendered will. He says, "No one can serve two masters. Either he will hate the one and love the other, or he will be devoted to the one and despise the other. You cannot serve both God and Money."

Money is not a neutral, impersonal medium of exchange. "Mammon" was the god of wealth in Carthage, the capital of Roman Africa. Money has all the characteristics of a pagan god. It seems to offer security, freedom, power, influence, status, and prestige. It is capable of inspiring devotion and it requires a single-minded preoccupation. It demands sacrifice and, ultimately, human sacrifice. Many sacrifice their health for money, through stress, long hours, and no exercise or relaxation. Worse still, some sacrifice the lives of others as human relationships are destroyed. No time is reserved for a spouse, children, friends, or God. "Drive! Push! Hustle! Scheme! Invest! Prepare! Anticipate! Work! 14-hour days . . . followed by weekends at the office, forfeited vacations, and midnight oil." [95] The result is often broken marriages and single-parent families—the latter created not only through divorce, but because one of the parents is always at work.

Jesus warns that we cannot serve two gods. Dietrich Bonhoeffer, the German theologian who was sentenced to death for opposing the Nazis, put it like this: "Our hearts have room only for one all-embracing devotion, and we can only cleave to one Lord." [96] Money is a good servant, but it is a bad master; if we serve it we will become a slave to it. Like sea water, the more you have the more you thirst for. John D. Rockefeller, founder of Standard Oil Company, was once asked, "How much money does it take to make someone happy?" He answered, "Just a little bit more than he has." Barry Humphries (a well known author in England) entitled his autobiography *More Please*. He wrote:

> I always wanted more. I never had enough milk, or money, or socks, or sex, or holidays, or first editions, or solitude, or gramophone records, or free meals, or real friends, or guiltless pleasure, or neckties, or applause, or unquestioning love, or persimmons. Of course, I have had more than my share of most of these commodities but it always left me with a vague feeling of unfulfillment: *where was the rest?*[97]

The problem with money is that we think we own it but, if we are not careful, it ends up owning us. We see an example of this in the film, *The Servant* in which James Fox stars as a man who employs a servant to look after him. Gradually he becomes more and more dependent on the servant (played by Dirk Bogarde), until eventually the servant dominates him. He ends up not having a servant, but being a slave to the man he thought was his servant. Henry Fielding pithily observed: "If you make money your god it will plague you like the devil."

In the ancient Roman port of Pompeii in the year A.D. 79, among those who fled from the torrents of lava erupting from Mount Vesuvius was a woman who sought to save not only her life, but also her valuable jewels. With her hands full of rings, bracelets, necklaces, chains, and other treasures she was overwhelmed by the rain of ashes from the volcano, and died. In the course of modern building operations outside the area of the buried city her petrified body was unearthed in a sea of jewels. She lost her life to save her treasure.

Jesus warns that if money is our God we will "despise" the only true God (vs. 24). The word for "despise" means "to be indifferent to or unconcerned about something." This is exactly what is happening to the church in the West today. As materialism has flourished, people have started to serve the god Mammon and have become apathetic and unconcerned about God. One of the thorns and thistles that Jesus describes in the parable of the sower is "the delight in riches." As this grows, it squeezes out life and the seed proves unfruitful.

Ultimately, materialism is atheism; it is to be without God. If, on the other hand, we serve God, we must be indifferent to and unconcerned about money. Indeed, we should be materially satisfied, since we are mere caretakers or stewards of our money, possessions, intelligence, and looks. We acknowledge before God that it all belongs to Him and we surrender all we have as an act of the will. When considering a major purchase, the issue should not simply be, "Have I got enough money?" (that would be serving the god Mammon), but, "Does God want me to have it?'

We should hold on to everything loosely. We should be like John Wesley, who when he heard that his house had been burned down exclaimed, "It is the Lord's house. Let Him see to it." That is freedom.

We break the power of materialism by generous and cheerful giving. Again, this is an act of the will, saying "no" to Mammon and "yes" to God. We cannot serve them both. Generous giving is an affront to Mammon and it destroys the demon greed. That demon will scream out, "You can't do this to me!" We should reply, "Yes I can, and I will!" and in doing so we kill it. Sometimes like a weed it reemerges and we have to kill it again by continuing to give generously. Generous giving celebrates "the fact that Jesus is Lord and Mammon isn't."[98]

14
How to Stop Worrying and Start Living 99
Matthew 6:25–34

²⁵ Therefore I tell you, do not worry about your life, what you will eat or drink; or about your body, what you will wear. Is not life more important than food, and the body more important than clothes? ²⁶ Look at the birds of the air; they do not sow or reap or store away in barns, and yet your heavenly Father feeds them. Are you not much more valuable than they? ²⁷ Who of you by worrying can add a single hour to his life?

²⁸ And why do you worry about clothes? See how the lilies of the field grow. They do not labor or spin. ²⁹ Yet I tell you that not even Solomon in all his splendor was dressed like one of these. ³⁰ If that is how God clothes the grass of the field, which is here today and tomorrow is thrown into the fire, will he not much more clothe you, O you of little faith? ³¹ So do not worry, saying, "What shall we eat?" or "What shall we drink?" or "What shall we wear?" ³² For the pagans run after all these things, and your heavenly Father knows that you need them. ³³ But seek first his kingdom and his righteousness, and all these things will be given to you as well. ³⁴ Therefore do not worry about tomorrow, for tomorrow will worry about itself. Each day has enough trouble of its own.

Some people are more prone to worry than others. Two cardiologists, Dr. Meyer Friedman and Dr. Ray Rosenman, after conducting research into the effects of stress upon the heart, divided people into Type A and Type B. Type A people were more prone to worry than Type B and they were found to be three times more likely to have a stroke or a heart attack than those in the Type B category, even if they were doing the same sort of work and living in similar conditions. Rob Parsons, Director of CARE for the Family, has identified some of the characteristics of Type A personalities.

We are very competitive. We compete over everything and find to our embarrassment that when playing board games with small children we are desperately trying to win.

We cannot resist a telephone ringing. The worst thing in life that can happen to us is to get to the telephone just as it stops ringing. If that happens we begin to call people, asking, "Was that you trying to reach me a moment ago?"

We swap lanes in traffic jams—even though we know that there is an eternal law that the lane we have just joined will now move more slowly than the lane we have just left.

When driving, we are constantly working out complicated mathematical equations: "Main street is 8 miles long. If I drive at 40 miles per hour it will take me five minutes, but there are stoplights, roughly two minutes wait at each. If I drive on the interstate, I bypass the stoplights, but must travel 15 miles, at 55 miles an hour, and there's always traffic which might slow me to 20 miles an hour. If I charter a helicopter . . . no, that's too difficult."

We hate stopping for gas. Why do we hate it so much? It's because when we pull in at the service station we look out over the road and see all the cars and trucks we had overtaken going past. [100]

Secular books and magazines offer various solutions to the problem of worry. Some give practical advice, such as more exercise and relaxation. Others are more bizarre. One women's magazine had an article on how to reduce your stress by half. It listed 10 instant "stress beaters." These ranged from ripping up magazines to beating up your pillow to sniffing a special blend of armpit and mammary gland secretion!

Whether or not these particular suggestions work, worry remains one of the most pervasive phenomena of our time.

The main worry Jesus is speaking about is material worry—that is, "what you will eat or drink . . . what you will wear" (vs. 25). Financial stress is at the heart of 70% of marital difficulties, but Jesus' teaching has wider application. He says, "Do not worry about your life." People are rarely without some kind of worry. There are the

159

day-to-day anxieties of exams, jobs, money, or houses, and the stress of difficult or broken relationships. People also worry about their health, the approach of old age and death, as well as the violence, immorality, and unpredictability of the society in which we live.

Jesus' solution to these worries is radical. As always, He did not merely deal with the symptoms but went to the root cause.

WHAT DOES HE MEAN?

When Jesus says, "Do not worry," what does He mean? The Greek word tells us not to be "anxious" or "unduly concerned." It is best defined by looking at what Jesus does not mean.

First, it does not mean that we should not think about the future. The King James Version's translation "take no thought" is misleading. The Greek word means "to take no anxious thought." It is not an excuse for a happy-go-lucky, irresponsible attitude to life. The book of Proverbs often makes it clear that planning is vital and we need to make prudent provision for the future. Indeed, one of the ways to avoid stress is to look ahead and plan.

Secondly, it is not an excuse for idleness. Jesus did not mean that we need not bother to earn a living.

160

We should not simply sit back and say, "God will provide." The birds of the air work extremely hard, but they are free from worry.

During Hudson Taylor's first missionary voyage to China in 1853, "when a violent storm off the Welsh coast threatened disaster," he felt it would be dishonoring to God to wear a life vest, so he gave his away. Later, however, he acknowledged his mistake: "The use of means ought not to lessen our faith in God, and our faith in God ought not to hinder our using whatever means He has given us for the accomplishment of His own purposes."[101]

Thirdly, He does not mean we should not be ambitious. Ambition is a strong desire to achieve success. It concerns our goals in life, and what secret inner motivation makes us tick. There is nothing wrong with ambition itself—as we shall see later.

Fourthly, Jesus is not saying that we should opt out of our responsibilities; we need to take responsibility for our own life, as one day we will have to give an account for it. Nor does it mean that we should not take responsibility for others. We have a duty to provide for our own family, as noted in the previous chapter, and we also have responsibilities to the world. We cannot disregard wars, racial prejudice, uneven distribution of wealth, the problems of AIDS and alcoholism. Nor can we disregard the personal problems of our neighbor. We are called to be agents to help others. We see this in the example of the apostle Paul. He worked hard, was imprisoned, flogged, exposed to death, stoned, shipwrecked and constantly in danger. He wrote, "I have labored and toiled and have often gone without sleep; I have known hunger and thirst and have often gone without food; I have been cold and naked. Besides everything else, I face daily the pressure of my concern for all the churches" (2 Corinthians. 11:27–28).

Fifthly, Jesus is not saying that we won't have anything to worry about. He never promised us a stress-free life; neither will we ever get rid of all the causes for worry. As soon as we get rid of one problem, others will move in to replace it. If anyone had cause for worry Jesus did. He faced the pressures of day-to-day living and had no regular source of income. He knew what it was for a close friend to die, He experienced the pressure of being misunderstood, threatened with death, and unfairly tried. He knew the pressure of powerful temptations, of suffering and living His life under the shadow of the cross. He knew He was to die on the cross for the sins of the world. The whole human race depended on Him. He is supremely qualified to say, "Do not worry," and to tell us why not.

WHY ARE WE NOT TO WORRY?

Jesus gives us seven reasons why we should not worry. First, to worry is to miss the point of life. Jesus says, "Therefore I tell you, do not worry about your life, what you will eat or drink; or about your body, what you will wear. Is not life more important than food, and the body more important than clothes?" (vs. 25). Life is far more important than material things. So often our worries are about relatively unimportant matters, such as food, drink, clothing, houses, and cars.

The magazine I mentioned earlier, with the article on stress-beaters, had another one entitled "Hedonism is surviving the recession-hit 90s." Much of the magazine was about the very things Jesus told us not to worry about—clothes, food, and drink. It included many advertisements about the body: how to shape it, how to "take four-and-a-half inches off without moving an inch" and how to make it attractive; how to "love your lips," and make them alluring, smooth, and more kissable; how to look younger, how to rejuvenate your skin and make it as soft as a baby's; how to feed it—"soups to be passionate about"; how to clothe it with lycra for "comfort, quality, and freedom" and silk scarves "to excite and inspire."

Jesus says that life is more important than these things. The columnist, Penny Perrick, wrote in *The Times*: "I have spent a fair bit of time this week wandering around the sales trying to pretend

162

I wanted something. What I want is true love, long eyelashes, and small feet and you can't buy any of those at Harrods." [102]

Elton John, commercially the most successful solo artist since Elvis Presley, has sold more than 200 million records and his earnings in 1994 were more than $25 million. Yet his drug-taking and eating disorders brought him misery. His suicide attempt during "Elton John week" in 1975 is well known. He sings on a recent album: "I had 40 years of pain and nothing to cling to." "My career was a success," he wrote, "but my life was pretty miserable."

Jesus says that if we simply seek external things we are missing the whole point of life. The point of life is to have a relationship with God through Jesus Christ.

Secondly, worry is illogical. Jesus says, "Look at the birds of the air; they do not sow or reap or store away in barns, and yet your heavenly Father feeds them. Are you not much more valuable than they?" (vs. 26).

" what a smug looking Robin "

Worry is a slander on God's character, suggesting that He is more interested in His pets than in His children. Birds are kept alive by food provided by nature, such as worms and insects. They have to spend a lot of time hunting and searching for the food, but it is there to be found. Jesus encourages us to look at them and to think about these facts.

Thirdly, worry is a complete waste of time. Jesus says, "Who of you by worrying can add a single hour to his life?" (vs. 27). Worry is futile, unproductive, and pointless. There is detailed discussion by theologians about whether Jesus meant that he could not add a "single cubit to his height" or "a single hour to his life," but it does not really matter which is right. The point Jesus is making is that we cannot add anything. Worry can only subtract from our lives by causing things like ulcers or a coronary thrombosis.

So many things we worry about never happen. Sir Winston Churchill said, "When I look back on all these worries, I remember the story of the old man who said on his death bed that he had had a lot of trouble in his life, most of which never happened." Mark Twain similarly reflected: "Most of my disasters never happened to me." William Barclay recalls the story of a London doctor who

> was paralyzed and bedridden, but almost outrageously cheerful, and his smile so brave and radiant that everyone forgot to be sorry for him. His children adored him, and when one of his boys was leaving the nest and setting forth on life's adventure, Dr. Greatheart gave him good advice: "Johnny," he said, "the thing to do, my lad, is to hold your own end up, and to do it like a gentleman, and please remember the biggest troubles you have got to face are those that never come." [103]

Fourthly, worry is incompatible with faith. Jesus says,

> And why do you worry about clothes? See how the lilies of the field grow. They do not labor or spin. Yet I tell you that not even Solomon in all his splendor was dressed like one of these. If that is how God clothes the grass of the field, which is here today and tomorrow is thrown into the fire, will he not much more clothe you, O you of little faith? (vss. 28–30).

Faith and anxiety are like fire and water. I once saw a poster outside a church which asked, "Why pray when you can worry and take tranquilizers?" Faith involves confidence in God's care and provision. To be a Christian is to walk in a trusting relationship with

God, but sin interferes with that relationship and often leads to worry.

Fifthly, worry is un-Christian. Jesus says, "For the pagans run after all these things, and your heavenly Father knows that you need them" (vs. 32). A primary concern with material needs is the characteristic of unbelievers, but we, through our trust in God, are called to be different.

Sixthly, worry is unnecessary. "But seek first his kingdom and his righteousness, and all these things will be given to you as well" (vs. 33). God promises to provide if we get our priorities right. Indeed, the Bible is full of such promises. For example, the psalmist says, "No good thing does he withhold from those whose walk is blameless" (Psalm 84:11). The apostle Paul also writes, "We know that in all things God works for the good of those who love him, who have been called according to his purpose" (Romans 8:28). Sometimes, as Paul knew only too well and Jesus experienced to the extreme, our situation may be difficult or painful. Yet God will work through adversity to better us in some way. The result may be increased intimacy with God, greater spiritual insight or far deeper faith with which to encourage and affirm others.

Seventhly, worry is incompatible with common sense. Jesus says, "Therefore do not worry about tomorrow, for tomorrow will worry about itself. Each day has enough trouble of its own" (vs. 34). We will have enough to worry about each day. God has given us our lives in units of 24 hours and we should take it a day at a time. We should live in "day-tight compartments." [104] Fiona Castle, who had to face the stress of her husband Roy Castle's battle against cancer, wrote at the end of her book *Give Us This Day*:

> Recently a friend commented to me that many people live their life as though it were a dress rehearsal for the real thing. But in fact, by tonight, we will have given the only performance of "today" that we will ever give. So we have to put our heart, our energy and honesty and sincerity into

what we do every day. As a show business family, we find that a very suitable illustration. And every show comes to the end of its run, when we must lay aside the costumes and step off the stage, into another, larger world.

So as we pray the prayer Jesus taught us, we ask God to "Give us this day"—thankfully receiving one day at a time—looking to Him to sustain us with everything we need, whether it be food, shelter, love of family and friends, or courage and hope to face the future. And at the same time we echo the words of the psalmist: "This is the day the Lord has made. We will rejoice and be glad in it" (Psalm 118:24). [105]

HOW DO WE STOP WORRYING?

Jesus tells us that the answer to worry is to "seek first his kingdom and his righteousness" (vs. 33). This will entail getting our ambitions and priorities right. Some of these are modest, such as food, drink, and clothing. Others are more grandiose: a bigger house, a new car, a better salary, reputation, fame, or power. But all these are self-centered and ultimately meaningless.

An article in the *Evening Standard* about the successful British TV and radio star, Chris Evans, asked, "So why isn't this man laughing?" It went on,

> On paper, Evans ought to be a happy man. He is just 27, his Channel 4 contract was said to be worth some $2 million a year, he has several marvelous cars, a splendid new apartment on Tower Bridge and a beautiful woman with whom to share it.
>
> But far from it, he seems quite depressed. "It hit me one Sunday morning," he explains, "that all I ever wanted was the 10:00 Saturday night slot on Channel 4 and now I'd achieved my life ambition at 27. So what do I do next?
>
> "You can compare it to climbing Everest. You climb it, and what do you do then? Climb the north face? OK, but so what? And then? Climb the north face with a grand piano over your shoulder? There has to be more to life. Finding out what that might be is the problem I've had ever since that Sunday. I haven't got any closer to working it out." [106]

Jesus says we need to change our priorities and our ambitions. It is not that we are to opt out, but quite the reverse. We are to take on a different set of responsibilities which are far more exciting and challenging. Jesus calls us to a nobler ambition—to seek His kingdom. We are to seek His rule and reign in our lives, our marriages, our home, family, and lifestyle. We are also to seek it in the lives of others—our friends, relations, neighbors, work colleagues, and in the community. We are to make the most of every opportunity.

One man who seems to have made the most of every opportunity in his life is Billy Graham, now in his late seventies. He has considered leaving his final sermon on tape, giving mourners a chance to respond to the gospel at his graveside. His message would start: "I'm not here in person today, I'm in Heaven. But I want to tell you, this is a wonderful place to be and if you want to come here you need to repent of your sins and come to Christ." [107]

Further, we are to seek God's "righteousness" in our lives and in society. We should seek to see His standards universally accepted, and invest our time, energy, and money in this pursuit. There are many men and women who, in God's strength, have made a great impact on the society around them. For example, William Wilberforce, as a Christian Member of Parliament, devoted his life to seeing God's standards in our society, campaigning for 45 years for the abolition of slavery. The necessary Act of Parliament was passed in July 1833, three days before he died.

As Christians today, we need to face up to poverty, the spread of AIDS, the breakdown of marriage, and the abuse of children, and determine to do something about them. Jesus promises that if we get our priorities and our ambitions right, then "all these things will be given to you as well" (i.e., all the little worries will be dealt with). Lesser ambitions are good, provided they are in second place. It is all right to want to be chairman of a major public company or to own a bank or to win Wimbledon, provided that these lesser ambitions serve greater, God-centered ambition.

Jesus says that if we take on His priorities and make them our greater ambition, then He will provide us with everything else we need.

The wealthy Baron Fitzgerald had only one son and heir, who died after leaving home. This was a tragedy from which the father never recovered. As his wealth increased, the Baron continued to invest in paintings by great masters, and when he died his will was found to call for all his paintings to be sold. Because of their quality and artistic value, messages were sent out to museums and collectors, advertising the sale.

When the day of the auction came, a large crowd assembled, and the lawyer read from Fitzgerald's will. It instructed that the first painting to be sold was that "of my beloved son." The portrait was by an unknown artist and it was of poor quality. The only bidder was an old servant who had known and loved the boy. For a small sum of money he bought it for its sentimental value and the memories it held for him. The attorney again read from the will, "Whoever buys my son gets all. The auction is over." [108]

Jesus said, "Seek first his kingdom and his righteousness, and all these things will be given to you as well" (vs. 33). That is how to stop worrying and start living.

15
How to Handle Criticism

Matthew 7:1–6

¹ Do not judge, or you too will be judged. ² For in the same way you judge others, you will be judged, and with the measure you use, it will be measured to you.

³ Why do you look at the speck of sawdust in your brother's eye and pay no attention to the plank in your own eye? ⁴ How can you say to your brother, "Let me take the speck out of your eye," when all the time there is a plank in your own eye? ⁵ You hypocrite, first take the plank out of your own eye, and then you will see clearly to remove the speck from your brother's eye.

⁶ Do not give dogs what is sacred; do not throw your pearls to pigs. If you do, they may trample them under their feet, and then turn and tear you to pieces.

One firm of lawyers in London has an unusual way of dealing with criticism. The staff are instructed to write as rude a reply as they can. They leave the letter on their desk overnight. When they arrive at work the next morning, they tear up the letter and send a polite, professional reply instead.

The French philosopher, Voltaire, wrote this response to a critical letter: "Dear Sir, I am sitting in the smallest room of my house. I have your letter of March 15th before me; soon it will be behind me. Your affectionate servant."

Thus far, Jesus has taught us about who we are (character), how we live (conduct), who we are when no one is looking (secret life), and what our desires are (ambitions). Now He moves on to how we respond to other people (relationships). We are not Christians on our own—we belong to a Christian community.

In this context Jesus teaches us how to handle criticism. He shows us how and when to give and receive it. He teaches us how to confront others and how to discriminate without judging.

THE COMMAND: WHAT ARE WE NOT TO DO? (VS. 1)

Jesus begins by saying to His disciples, "Do not judge" (vs. 1). Some have taken this as a blanket command that prevents Christians from making any kind of judgments at all.

"I'm afraid I cannot comment on the weather"

However, Jesus' words must not be taken out of context. We have to look at the immediate setting of the Sermon on the Mount (see, for example, vs. 6 and vss.15–20), Jesus' teaching as a whole (e.g., Matthew 10:14–15; 18:15–17), and the rest of the Bible.

First, we must look at what Jesus does *not* mean. He is not talking here about the authority of the state. Jesus recognized that even Pilate had a God-given right to judge. Pilate's power was given to him "from above" (John 19:11). In a fallen world we need judges. The apostle Paul describes a judge as "God's servant to do you good. But if you do wrong, be afraid, for he does not bear the sword for nothing. He is God's servant, an agent of wrath to bring punishment on the wrongdoer" (Romans 13:4).

Nor is Jesus talking about the exercise of authority in the home or in the church. The book of Proverbs is full of exhortations to parents to exercise authority in the home. This is a kind of judging, but it is a right kind of judging. Discipline is also necessary in the church. One definition of the church, at the time of the Reformation, was "a place in which the word is preached, the sacraments are administered, and discipline is exercised." This is in line with New Testament teaching. In the Pastoral Epistles, Timothy, as a church leader, is told to "correct, rebuke and encourage—with great patience and careful instruction" (2 Timothy 4:2). Paul himself was not afraid of making judgments when it came to false teaching (Galatians 1:8–9; 2:11; 5:12).

In 1 Corinthians, Paul stresses the need for the church to deal with immorality and to pass judgment on those in the church who are guilty of serious sin (1 Corinthians 5). We are in no position to judge those outside, but we have a duty to judge those inside: "I have already passed judgment on the one who did this, just as if I were present. . . . What business is it of mine to judge those outside the church? Are you not to judge those inside? God will judge those outside. 'Expel the wicked man from among you'" (1 Corinthians 5:3, 12–13). Disputes between believers are not to be taken to unbelievers, but should be judged, if necessary, by the church (1 Corinthians 6:1–6).

Further, as individual Christians we need to exercise judgment and we should not suspend our critical faculties. If we are not to throw our "pearls to pigs" (vs. 6) we need to discern who the pigs are. Jesus also warns us to watch out for false prophets (vss.15–20). We are required to distinguish the false from the true and use the test Jesus lays down: "By their fruit you will recognize them" (vss.16, 20). There is indeed a right kind of judgment. After healing a man on the Sabbath, Jesus said to the Jews: "Stop judging by mere appearances, and make a right judgment" (John 7:24). We are encouraged to "test the spirits" (1 John 4:1) and even to "test everything"

(1 Thessalonians 5:21). Most of us will be required at times to make value judgments, to choose between different policies and plans of action. None of these judgments by the courts, parents, church leaders, or individual Christians is forbidden by Jesus.

We have looked at what Jesus does *not* mean. But what does He mean? Surely what Jesus is attacking here is a judgmental attitude toward other people. He is warning that we must not judge harshly, condemning others with censorious and harsh criticism. We are not to set ourselves up as God, and judge our fellow men and women when we are in no position to do so. We are not to magnify the errors and weaknesses of others and make the worst of them. We are not to be fault-finders who are negative and destructive toward other people and enjoy actively seeking out their failures. As Martyn Lloyd-Jones put it: "If we ever know the feeling of being rather pleased when we hear something unpleasant about another, that is the wrong spirit." [109]

We are not to have the self-righteous attitude of the Pharisees "who were confident of their own righteousness and looked down on everybody else" (Luke 18:9), which Jesus illustrated with the parable of the Pharisee and the tax collector. We are not to despise others and regard them with contempt.

172

This applies to all our fellow human beings, whether they are Christians or not. We are not to adopt a superior attitude of unqualified condemnation to those who are not Christians.

I'm saved and you're not.

As Christians, we have received mercy. We have Christ's righteousness, not our own, and so we have no cause for pride. We should not patronize non-Christians or, worse still, judge and condemn them. If this applies to those who are not Christians, how much more should it apply to our "brother."

THE REASON: WHY ARE WE NOT TO JUDGE? (VSS. 1–2)

Jesus also gives us the reason why we should not judge. The command not to judge is followed by a warning: ". . . or you too will be judged. . . . And with the measure you use, it will be measured to you" (vss. 1–2). To use courtroom language, if we attempt to occupy the bench we will end up the defendant. We will be our own judges. As we judge, we are judged.

While a comment on a work of art may or may not be fair judgment, it will expose the extent of the critic's knowledge. One visitor to our church told me he was a well-known artist and would really like me to go and look at his paintings because he wanted to know my assessment of them. As his studio was close to the church,

I went to have a look. What I know about modern art could be written on a very small postage stamp, but I tried to sound as knowledgeable as I could.

I thought I was doing quite well until we were looking at a piece of burlap with something stuck on it. He said, "What do you think of this?"

I asked, "Is this the back of the painting?"

"Don't be ridiculous! This is it," he said, and then proceeded to explain to me the significance of the work, and as he did so I gradually began to understand how powerful it was. But my ignorance had been fully revealed. In my attempt to judge, I had in fact been judged! The incident showed me that when we sit in judgment on others we inevitably reveal ourselves, with our critical spirits, our pettiness, our insecurities, and our attempts to build ourselves up by knocking others down.

Not only will we be our own judges, but we will bring the judgment of others on our own heads. If we judge, we will be judged with equal harshness by others. Those who judge must expect similar treatment. In the end we will create an environment of judgmentalism, and this is a tragedy when it occurs in the church. It can be the leader who is judgmental of others, or the congregation who have "roast preacher for Sunday lunch." Nothing empties churches faster than this kind of atmosphere. We try to avoid critical people because, deep down, we suspect that if they are critical of others then they are probably equally critical of us when our backs are turned. Eventually, a self-appointed judge finds that the only person with whom he can associate is himself. If we object to others sitting in judgment on us, we should not sit in judgment on them.

Yet when Jesus says, "Do not judge or you too will be judged," He is probably thinking not so much of our own judgment, or the judgment of others, as He is of the judgment of God. (Although the first two may be an outworking of the third.) The passive tense of the Greek verb suggests that God is the agent of this judgment, as we have also seen in Matthew 6:14–15, 18, 23–25.

Only God is qualified to judge. We would be wise not to usurp the prerogative of the Judge of all the earth, because we are hopelessly ill-equipped to do so. No human being is qualified to sit in judgment on another. In fact, one root of sin is to want to be judge over others. Genesis 3 tells us that the serpent tempted Adam and Eve with the words, "You will be like God, knowing good and evil" (Genesis 3:5). The root of sin is a desire to be like God, of which one aspect is to be judge over others. Jesus liberates us from this because He is the Judge and takes the burden of it from us. For a start, none of us is good enough to do so, as we are all sinners. As Paul puts it:

> You, therefore, have no excuse, you who pass judgment on someone else, for at whatever point you judge the other, you are condemning yourself, because you who pass judgment do the same things. Now we know that God's judgment against those who do such things is based on truth. So when you, a mere man, pass judgment on them and yet do the same things, do you think you will escape God's judgment? (Romans 2:1–3).

Secondly, we are all full of prejudice, however much we might like to think of ourselves as unbiased and objective. A friend of mine works for a leading firm of certified accountants and he is involved in recruiting trainees from universities. As part of his interview training course, he was asked to fill in a piece of paper. Above the center line, he was asked to list the prejudices he thought he might have and below it the prejudices he saw in others that he didn't have. All the interviewers were asked to do the same. The result was that above the line they listed trivial matters, but below the line they put down major prejudices like racism, sexism, size, and looks. Faced with this total mismatch they had to recognize that perhaps they too had major prejudices.

Thirdly, we never know all the facts. Only God knows what is "hidden in darkness" and "the motives of men's hearts" (1 Corinthians 4:5). He is the only one who is qualified to judge and will take into account what we so often do not—for example, the advantages that some have of Christian homes and easy-going dispositions, and the disadvantages others have in terms of background and temperament. In due time the Lord will judge. As Paul writes: "It is the Lord who judges me. Therefore judge nothing before the appointed time; wait till the Lord comes. He will bring to light what is hidden in darkness and will expose the motives of men's hearts" (1 Corinthians 4:4–5).

We will be judged by our own yardstick. Some rabbis used to teach that God had two measures: a measure of justice and a measure of mercy. We get the choice, depending on which we use to judge others. If we insist on justice, justice is what we ourselves will receive. But if we are merciful, then we will receive God's mercy. As Christians, we have experienced the extraordinary mercy and forgiveness of God as He pours out His love and His grace on us. He constantly forgives and He does not treat us as our sins deserve. If this is how God treats us, surely we ought to treat our brothers and sisters in the same way. We are called to love as He loves us; to "believe all things" and "to hope all things" (1 Corinthians 13:7, RSV). We should always give others the benefit of the doubt and be constantly forgiving, understanding, and loving.

THE ILLUSTRATION: WHAT DOES IT MEAN IN PRACTICE? (VSS. 3–6)

Jesus illustrates the point by using a metaphor from a carpenter's workshop. "Why do you look at the speck of sawdust in your brother's eye and pay no attention to the plank in your own eye? How can you say to your brother, 'Let me take the speck out of your eye,' when all the time there is a plank in your own eye?" (vss. 3–5).

Jesus often referred to the Pharisees as "blind guides." A man with a plank of wood in his eye is totally blind, yet he is trying to take a tiny splinter of wood from someone else's eye.

Again, it is important to see what Jesus is not saying. He is not ruling out constructive criticism. True criticism of literature, art, and music involves a high exercise of the human mind. It should never be merely destructive, but constructive and appreciative. In a similar way all training involves constructive criticism. A teacher needs to criticize his or her pupils constructively if they are to learn. The teacher too will have received constructive criticism during training. We cannot object to the criticism of the teacher or coach, as it improves our skills and builds us up. Without it, any kind of learning would be impossible. Indeed, I for one am very grateful to the many people who have given me constructive criticism over the years.

One of the greatest preachers of the nineteenth century, Charles Haddon Spurgeon, said to his students:

> Get a friend to tell you your faults, or better still, welcome an enemy who will watch you keenly and sting you savagely. What a blessing such an irritating critic will be to a wise man, what an intolerable nuisance to a fool! Correct yourself diligently and frequently, or you will fall into errors unawares, false tones will grow, and slovenly habits will form insensibly; therefore criticize yourself with unceasing care. [110]

This illustration given by Jesus is not aimed at loving, constructive criticism, but at unkind and hypocritical criticism, even if it takes the form of a kindly act. The splinter comes from the same plank that the critic has in his own eye. That is why Jesus says, "You hypocrite" (vs. 5). Hypocrisy is the gap between what we show on the outside and what we know is true on the inside. Indeed, the things we criticize in other people are often the things we see in ourselves. By criticism, we build ourselves up. Speaking ill of others is a way of dishonestly speaking well of ourselves. There is a double standard in having "a

"Tut, Hilda bought another dress yesterday"

rosy view of ourselves and a jaundiced view of others,"[111] for we point the accusing finger at others, but never turn it on ourselves. It makes us feel better to gloat over the sins and errors of others—hence our love of scandals. We lap up all the sordid details and every speck we collect helps us ignore the log-jam in our own eye.

This applies not only to the moral faults of others, but also to doctrinal ones as well. Some doctrinal critics may agree with 99% of their opponent's view. We may agree on the Trinity, the person and work of Jesus Christ, the nature of the atonement, the authority of Scripture, and issues of morality, but we find what is objectively a minor area of disagreement and latch onto it. We feel that we are not "sound" unless we are constantly denouncing and condemning. So we write with poisoned pens. Could it be that we are blinded by the log in our own eye? Often we are defensive, rigid, judgmental, intolerant, and even nasty and petty. Unless we first remove the plank of hypercriticism and censoriousness from our own eyes, we will not see clearly to remove the splinter from the eyes of others.

Jesus, as we have seen, does not rule out all criticism of others. But we need to start with self-criticism. As John Stott puts it, "We need to be as critical of ourselves as we often are of others, and as generous to others as we always are to ourselves."[112] Jesus says that when we have removed the plank we will be able to see clearly to help others (vs. 5).

Once we have removed the plank we will be able to act in love. We need to clean up our act first. If we are so concerned about righteousness, purity, and sound doctrine, we should model it first. Then we would be in a position to help others in a genuinely loving way.

It is no accident that Jesus uses the analogy of an eye. "There is no organ that is more sensitive than the eye. The moment the finger touches it, it closes up."[113] Criticism of others is a delicate operation. If we are to criticize another person, we should do so not in a condemning way, but with humility, understanding, sympathy, and generosity. We should be like a mother who notices a speck in her child's eye and very carefully and delicately takes it out. Confrontation should be combined with affirmation. As Paul writes to Timothy: "Correct, rebuke and encourage—with great patience and careful instruction" (2 Timothy 4:2).

We see how Jesus sets out the procedure for confrontation of sin in Matthew 18:15–17. It starts with a person-to-person encounter (vs. 15). We should always endeavor to meet face-to-face, and not to criticize publicly or behind someone's back. There should be no sense of superior attitude or degrading the other person. If the first step fails, the second step is to get certain other people involved. In this situation, the community as a group has a right to pronounce judgment. The purpose is not to destroy, but to bring someone back to repentance and restoration. We should never criticize unless we can do so in genuine love for our brother or sister.

QUALIFICATION: ARE THERE ANY LIMITS? (VS. 6)

The next verse seems incongruous and almost contradicts what has gone before. Jesus says, "Do not give dogs what is sacred; do not throw your pearls to pigs. If you do, they may trample them under their feet, and then turn and tear you to pieces" (vs. 6). Jesus is in fact warning of the opposite of judgmentalism: the danger of being indiscriminate. So He limits the range of the command "do not judge" (vs. 1) and qualifies the apparently absolute prohibition.

As Christians, we have been entrusted with something that is "sacred." The valuable "pearls" are the truth of the message concerning the kingdom of God and the good news of the Gospel. Yet not everyone sees its value. Some human beings act like animals. The word for "dogs" does not mean cuddly household pets, but wild hounds and mongrels that roam the streets and scavenge the city's rubbish dumps. "Pigs" were unclean animals to the Jews, and would have been more like wild hogs than our cultivated varieties of pig. The picture Jesus paints then is of a man trying to feed such swine with precious pearls. Not surprisingly they find these pearls hard to chew, tasteless, and unable to satisfy their appetites! In rage the animals spit them out and turn on the man, tearing him to pieces.

Jesus is not suggesting, of course, that we should avoid preaching the Gospel to unbelievers, for that is exactly what He commissioned His followers to do. Rather, He is warning that there are some who show what Calvin described as a "hardened contempt for God." They have had ample opportunity to respond, but have defiantly rejected the Gospel. Jesus is saying that there comes a point when we should not persist any further. Later on He tells His disciples: "If anyone will not welcome you or listen to your words, shake the dust off your feet when you leave that home or town" (Matthew 10:14; see also Luke 10:10–11). We cannot force the Gospel on people—that was the mistake of the Inquisition! Neither should we waste time with those who simply want to mock, argue, or ridicule.

Paul followed this policy in Pisidian Antioch when the Jews reject-ed the Gospel. Paul said: "We had to speak the word of God to you first. Since you reject it and do not consider yourselves worthy of eternal life, we now turn to the Gentiles" (Acts 13:46). Likewise in

Corinth, he said, "Your blood be on your own heads! I am clear of my responsibility. From now on I will go to the Gentiles" (Acts 18:6).

Of course, many of us start out by mocking, arguing, and ridiculing. I certainly did. I am very grateful that people did not give up on me right away. Again, love is the key to knowing when to stop. Sometimes it is more loving to persist, but at other times it is more loving to stop if we are doing more harm than good.

This principle of Jesus in verse 6 also warns us to be careful ourselves not to be like the "dogs" and "pigs" in rejecting the truth. The truth can hurt when it comes in the form of criticism. If we respond like the "dogs" and "pigs" it will stop others from giving us good advice. But, "Like an earring of gold or an ornament of fine gold is a wise man's rebuke to a listening ear" (Proverbs 25:12).

In conclusion, Jesus is urging us to act with love and charity toward our fellow human beings. On October 31, 1991, Frederick Chiluba, President of Zambia, took power in the country's first democratic elections, achieving a landslide victory over Kenneth Kaunda. President Chiluba's first act was to call for a celebration of praise and to establish a covenant with God on behalf of his people. He confessed the country's immorality, bribery, and corruption, and asked for forgiveness through the blood of Jesus. He prayed for healing, restoration, revival, and blessing.

Chiluba, a former trade unionist, had been arrested and detained in 1981 by Kaunda's government. In prison he read the New Testament three times in three months and to use his own words, "The Lord hit me on the head." When Jimmy Carter came to monitor the elections he said to Chiluba, "Do you realize you could be President tomorrow? What you say today will matter tomorrow. Every word you utter should have meaning."

Chiluba asked, "What do you mean? I have been attacked."

Carter replied, "It doesn't matter. It is not the attacks that will win the elections, but the issues. The more you respect the person who attacks you, the more reasonable people will think you are."

Chiluba replied, "What a coincidence. Here is Jimmy Carter and here is the Bible. He must have been sent by God." Chiluba went on to say, "You should have seen the joy and delight in the hearts of the people when there was no violence. In fact I said, 'Let us just wish Dr. Kaunda a nice farewell, but no attacks, no insults, nothing.' And that was marvelous. That is the work of God."

The message of reconciliation with his opponents brought one of the most peaceful days ever in the history of that country. He was swept to power in a celebration of democracy, freedom, and a new beginning. The celebration of praise following the elections was unparalleled in the history of the country and Chiluba's non-judgmental attitude brought unity to the country.

How much more should we have this same attitude in the church. We need to follow the words of Jesus and cut out our petty squabbles and our judgmentalism. We need to stop criticizing other denominations and other traditions within our own denominations. We need to forget the past, drop the labels, and unite around the person of Jesus Christ. We need to get on with the task that He has given us until He comes again. Then He will do the judging and His judgment will be perfect.

16
How to Get Our Relationships Right

Matthew 7:7–12

⁷ Ask and it will be given to you; seek and you will find; knock and the door will be opened to you. ⁸ For everyone who asks receives; he who seeks finds; and to him who knocks, the door will be opened.

⁹ Which of you, if his son asks for bread, will give him a stone? ¹⁰ Or if he asks for a fish, will give him a snake? ¹¹ If you, then, though you are evil, know how to give good gifts to your children, how much more will your Father in heaven give good gifts to those who ask him! ¹² So in everything, do to others what you would have them do to you, for this sums up the Law and the Prophets.

Lee began his life with a whole host of disadvantages. His mother was a powerfully built, domineering woman who found it difficult to love anyone. She had been married three times and her second husband divorced her because she beat him up regularly. Lee's father was her third husband; he died of a heart attack two months before Lee was born. As a consequence, his mother had to work long hours from his earliest childhood.

She gave him no affection, love, discipline, or training during those early years. She even forbade him to call her at work. Other children had little to do with him, so he was alone most of the time. He was absolutely rejected from his earliest childhood. He was poor and untrained and unlovable. When he was 13 years old, a school psychologist commented that he probably didn't even know the meaning of the word "love." During adolescence, the girls would have nothing to do with him and he fought with the boys.

Despite a high IQ, he failed academically and finally dropped out during his third year of high school. He thought he might find acceptance in the Marine Corps; they reportedly built "men," and he wanted to be one. But his problems went with him. The other marines ridiculed him and he fought back. He continually resisted authority, was court-martialed and thrown out with a dishonorable discharge. So there he was, a young man in his early twenties, absolutely friendless and shipwrecked. He was small and scrawny in stature and had an adolescent squeak in his voice. He had no talent, no skill, no sense of self-worth.

Again he decided to run from his problems, and left America to live abroad. There he married a woman who had herself been an illegitimate child, and he brought her back to America. Soon she began to display the same contempt for him that everyone else had. Although they had two children, he never enjoyed the status and respect of being a father. His marriage began to crumble as his wife demanded things that he could not provide. Instead of being his ally against a bitter world, as he had hoped, she became his most vicious opponent. She could outfight him and she learned to bully him, on one occasion even locking him in the bathroom as a punishment. Finally, she threw him out.

He then tried to make it on his own, but he was terribly lonely. After days of solitude, he went home and begged her to take him back. He surrendered any vestige of pride; he crawled, he accepted humiliation, he came back on her terms. Despite his meager salary, he presented her with $78, asking her to take it and spend it any way she wished. But she laughed at him and belittled his feeble attempts to supply the family's needs. She ridiculed his failure. She made fun of his sexual impotency in front of a friend. At one point, when the darkness of his private nightmare threatened to envelop him, he fell on his knees and wept bitterly.

Finally, in silence, he pleaded no more. No one wanted him. No one had ever wanted him. His ego lay shattered in fragments.

The next day, he was a strangely different man. He got up, went to the garage and took a rifle he had hidden there. He carried it with him to his newly-acquired job at a book-storage building. And, from a window on the third floor of that building, shortly after noon on November 22nd, 1963, he sent two shells crashing into the head of President John Fitzgerald Kennedy.

Lee Harvey Oswald, the rejected, unlovable failure, killed the man who, more than any other man on earth, embodied all the success, beauty, wealth, and family affection which he lacked.[114]

Lee Harvey Oswald was a classic case of a casualty caused by a breakdown in relationships, which is so prevalent in our society. Four out of ten marriages end in divorce and one in four children is born outside marriage. One in three children grows up without a father. The Chief Rabbi, Jonathan Sacks, puts it like this:

> The story of the late twentieth century is one of the displacement of the community by the State and hence of the replacement of morality by politics. That is why our moral agenda has changed. Our concerns—with inequality and injustice, war and famine and ecology—go deep. But these are issues to be addressed to governments. We are willing to make sacrifices on their behalf. We join protests, sign petitions, send donations. But these are large scale and for the most part impersonal problems. They have relatively little to do with what morality was traditionally largely about: the day-to-day conduct between neighbors and strangers, what Martin Buber called the "I-and-Thou" dimension of our lives. Instead, in our personal relationships we believe in autonomy, the right to live our lives as we choose.[115]

Relationships are the most important aspect of our lives. As Jesus comes toward the end of the ethical teaching in the Sermon on the Mount, before the call to commitment, He summarizes all that He has been saying: "For this sums up the Law and the Prophets" (vs. 12). This section of the Sermon on the Mount sums up not only the sermon itself, but also the Ten Commandments, the law of Moses, and all the ethical teaching of the Bible.

In this section He summarizes how to get our relationships with God and with other people right. Later on in the Gospel, He makes the same points in a slightly different way. One of the Pharisees asks Him this question: "Teacher, which is the greatest commandment in the Law?" Jesus replies: " 'Love the Lord your God with all your heart and with all your soul and with all your mind.' This is the first and greatest commandment. And the second is like it: 'Love your neighbor as yourself.' All the Law and the Prophets hang on these two commandments" (Matthew. 22:36–40).

HOW TO GET OUR RELATIONSHIP WITH GOD RIGHT (VSS. 7–11)

The first and greatest commandment is to love God with all our hearts, souls and minds. Here, Jesus puts it slightly differently. He says we are to "ask . . . seek . . . knock." The tense of the Greek verbs is the present imperative. Literally it means "to keep on asking, to keep on seeking, and to keep on knocking." We need to realize our need for God and His gifts and then to seek Him with persistence and perseverance. We are not to be like those who make a New Year's resolution and within a few weeks have failed to keep it. Nor are we to be like the small boys who knock on a door and then run away. We need to press in with a burning, wholehearted pursuit of God. God promises, "You will seek me and find me when you seek me with all your heart. I will be found by you" (Jeremiah 29:13–14). As we "ask . . . seek . . . knock" Jesus promises that we will receive, find, and "the door will be opened" (vs. 8).

How is it that we can be so confident in this relationship? This passage reveals three reasons to us. First, God is our "Father in heaven" (vs. 11). He is the one whom Jesus taught us to address as "Abba." After examining the extensive prayer literature of ancient Judaism, Professor Jeremias wrote that "in no place in this immense literature is this invocation of God as *Abba* to be found. . . . *Abba* was an everyday word, a homely family word. No Jew would have dared to address

187

God in this manner. Jesus did it always . . . and authorizes His disciples to repeat the word Abba after Him."[116]

Jonathan Cavan became a Christian while taking the Alpha course at Holy Trinity Brompton, and his life changed dramatically. As a young and successful businessman he traveled around the world. On one particular journey he decided to write to his father for the first time in a long while, but never finished the letter because he started to talk to his neighbor about Jesus.

Later on he was explaining to Helena, his fiancée, how he communicated with others in business by using Microsoft's electronic E-mail. He had a laptop computer at home and he created an E-mail message. He showed her how he was able to communicate with different people all over the world at the same time. He created an E-mail and addressed it to all the general managers at Microsoft, all the sales managers at Microsoft worldwide, all the sales people who look after banks worldwide and to Bill Gates, the chairman of the organization. Then he demonstrated how he could embed documents into E-mail. As an example, he embedded the unfinished letter he had been writing to his father on the plane.

He thought no more of it until one month later a woman in his group at work borrowed his laptop, plugged it into the corporate network and received the message: "You have an unsent message. Would you like to send it?" She clicked "yes" and that message hit the desktops of over 500 senior managers and executives in that corporation. Jonathan did not realize it until he got a phone call later.

At first he was very worried about it, but then he reread the letter. It went like this:

Dear Dad,
At last I am writing to you. I have thought about you almost daily. I have not written because I have known that I could not write without saying something that would challenge your thinking and tug at your heart. However, my words aim to be an encouragement.

I am playing soccer weekly and play in a team which is doing well; we won our last game 9–1. I have a vitality for life that makes me feel fitter, stronger, happier, and more peaceful than ever before. God is restoring the lost years. Many people at Microsoft really do not have a life outside work. The organization plays an unhealthy central role to their existence. By worldly standards this may appear not a bad option . . . but it is absolutely no comparison to having Jesus Christ as central to one's existence as He is to mine. He lives inside me and He is able to guide every one of my thoughts, words, and deeds if I am obedient to His will.

Do you know how much I craved to speak to you, soft heart to soft heart, even during my most rebellious years? For so many years we have communicated mask to mask. . . .

He received some interesting responses, including two from Bill Gates, Chairman of the company. He also received a message from a director in Canada, saying his father had died one month previously and that he had never known a son to speak so lovingly to his father and that he had cried there in his office. A message of encouragement and support came from the president of Microsoft Europe, and one of his colleagues came into the office, confessing that he had left the Lord and now wanted to return as a result of reading the letter.

This incident shows how powerful the relationship between a human father and son can be. How much more powerful and crucial is our relationship with our Father in heaven.

The second reason for pursuing God with all our hearts is that if we seek God, we will receive "good gifts" (vs. 11). So often we fear that if we pursue God wholeheartedly we will miss out on something good and get a raw deal. But God loves us. Therefore, we can be sure we will receive "good gifts." Jesus, using an *a fortiori* argument ("how much more" vs. 11), assures us that God will never give us anything harmful. He says, "Which of you, if his son asks for bread, will give him a stone? Or if he asks for a fish, will give him a snake? If you, then, though you are evil, know how to give good gifts to your

189

children, how much more will your Father in heaven give good gifts to those who ask him!" (vss. 7–11).

Bread and fish were the two most common foods around the Sea of Galilee. It is possible that a round limestone might look like a loaf of bread. They have the same shape and color. The eel-like catfish of the Sea of Galilee might look like a snake, but no earthly father would be so cruel to his children as to give them stones instead of bread or snakes instead of fish. It is even more absurd to imagine that God would give us anything harmful. Because we know that God is our loving heavenly Father, promises of answered prayer are not blank checks. If they were, we would hardly dare pray. But because He loves us, God will only give us "good gifts."

Yet all human fathers are intrinsically "evil." This is a comparative statement. Compared with God, all of us, even kind parents, are evil. Yet even evil people do good things sometimes. Odette Hallowes, wartime heroine famous through the film *Odette*, died at age 82 in March 1995. *The Times* obituary, after detailing some of her extraordinary acts of courage, added that there was also publicity of a more lighthearted kind.

> On one occasion her mother's house in Kensington was burgled, the thief making off with some silver spoons, and Odette's George Cross and Legion d'Honneur. Distraught at the loss of her daughter's treasures, Mme. Brailly appealed through the press for their return. The thief, evidently a humane soul, obliged. His letter accompanying the decorations read: "You, Madame, appear to be a dear old lady. God bless you and your children. I thank you for having faith in me. I am not all that bad—it's just circumstances. Your little dog really loves me. I gave him a nice pat and left him a piece of meat. Sincerely yours, A Bad Egg." [117]

If even bad eggs do good things, how much more will our Father in heaven do things.

Thirdly, we can be confident in seeking God, because God will *only* give us good things. It would be a terrible thing if God always gave us what we asked for, as we would never be able to pray with confidence. We would always be afraid of making an awful blunder.

> The Greeks had their stories about the gods who answered men's prayers, but the answer was an answer with a barb in it, a double-edged gift. Aurora, the goddess of the dawn, fell in love with Tithonus, a mortal youth, so the Greek story ran. Zeus, the king of the gods, offered her any gift that she might choose for her mortal lover. Aurora very naturally chose that Tithonus might live forever; but she had forgotten to ask that Tithonus might remain forever young; and so Tithonus grew older and older and older and could never die and the gift became a curse. [118]

How different is our heavenly Father from other gods. Good fathers always correct their children's blunders. C. H. Spurgeon once said: "Our prayers go to heaven in a revised version." That is why Martyn Lloyd-Jones wrote:

> I thank God that He is not prepared to do anything that I may chance to ask Him, and I say that as the result of my own past experience. In my past life I, like all others, have often asked God for things, and have asked God to do things, which at that time I wanted very much and which I believed were the very best things for me. But now, standing at this particular juncture in my life and looking back, I say that I am profoundly grateful to God that He did not grant me certain things for which I asked, and that He shut certain doors in my face. At the time I did not understand, but I know now, and am grateful to God for it. So I thank God that this is not a universal promise, and that God is not going to grant me my every desire and request. God has a much better way for us. [119]

God will not give us things which are not good for us or for others, directly or indirectly, immediately or ultimately. What He promises here is that God will answer when we ask for good gifts.

We can pray with confidence because God does not make mistakes. He is a generous God who gives "good gifts." He gives us "everything we need for life and godliness" (2 Peter 1:3). This should be our primary aim in life: to develop a relationship with our loving heavenly Father; to love Him; to seek and to receive good gifts from His fatherly hand; to love Him with all our heart, mind, soul, and strength.

HOW TO GET OUR RELATIONSHIPS WITH OTHER PEOPLE RIGHT (VS. 12)

So much unhappiness and suffering in the world is due to relationships that are not right—the breakdown of relationships between nations, races, religions, neighbors, friends, husbands and wives, parents and children. Recently I followed the newspaper reports of an 11-day hearing at Barnstaple county court between two neighbors. One of the parties had kept a record of the dispute and his diary contained nearly 1,000 entries by the time it reached court. The cost of the court case was over $75,000, and all because of a petty dispute. As Jesus comes to the end of His ethical teaching from the Sermon on the Mount, He summarizes all He has taught.

In verse 12, the Sermon on the Mount reaches its summit. This saying is the climax of all Jesus' ethical teaching and is the most universally famous thing Jesus ever said. It is the topmost peak of social ethics. It is said that Emperor Alexander Severus had it written in gold on his wall and it has become known as "the golden rule."

Many people have taught the negative version of this rule. Confucius said, "What you do not want done to yourself, do not do to others." The Stoics said, "What you do not wish to be done to you, do not do to anyone else." Epictetus said, "What you avoid suffering yourself, seek not to inflict on others." The Old Testament Apocrypha said, "And what you hate, do not do to anyone" (Tobit 4:15, RSV). Rabbi Hillel (c. 20 B.C.) was challenged by a heathen who said that he was prepared to convert to Judaism if Rabbi Hillel was able to teach the whole law while standing on one leg. Hillel replied, "What is hateful to yourself, do to no other; that is the whole law and the rest is commentary. Go and learn."

Jesus was the first to formulate this positively. Nowhere in ancient literature is there a parallel to the positive form in which Jesus puts it. The positive is far more searching. The negative says, "I won't do anyone any harm," which allows us to be inactive. This is often the philosophy of the world. Many feel they are not "sinners" because they do not kill or rob or deliberately harm others. But followers of Jesus Christ are called to something far higher. We are called to say not only, "I won't do anyone any harm," but also, "I will go out of my way to help." There is no permission to withdraw into a world where we offend no one but do not accomplish any positive good. For example, it is not enough that we do not break up marriages; we must also help to put them back together. It is not enough not to steal; we must give generously. It is not enough not to harm our neighbors; we must also positively help them.

Jesus recognizes that self-love is a powerful force in our lives. We are self-centered, self-protective, and self-concerned. Jesus challenges us to love others as much as we love ourselves. We are to ask the question: "How would I like to be treated in that situation?" As J. C. Ryle once commented:

> This is a golden rule indeed! It does not merely forbid all petty malice and revenge, all cheating and overreaching: it does much more. It settles a hundred difficult points, which in a world like this are continually arising between man and man; it prevents the necessity of laying down endless little rules for our conduct in specific cases, it sweeps the whole debatable ground with one mighty principle; it shows us a balance and measure, by which everyone may see at once what is his duty. Is there a thing we would not like our neighbor to do to us? Then let us always remember that this is the thing we ought not to do to him. Is there a thing we would like him to do to us? Then this is the very thing we ought to do to him—How many intricate questions would be decided at once if this rule were honestly used![120]

Jesus says that "this sums up the Law and the Prophets" (vs. 12). He does not say that it replaces or abolishes them. We need details to keep us from sentimentalism, but we need general principles to keep us from legalism lest we forget the spirit of the rules. We are not to be obsessed by the rules and regulations, nor to obey them mechanically. The rules are not detached, impersonal, or negative, but their whole purpose is so that we may love our neighbor as ourselves. Every detailed regulation is simply an illustration of the great central principle that Jesus teaches here.

If everyone acted on this rule, there would be no slavery, war, robbery or lying—only justice and love. It would lead to the transformation of society. As Rabbi Jonathan Sacks sums up: "The more law is inscribed upon our hearts, the less it needs to be policed in the streets." [121] The universal practice of this rule now by all professing Christians would carry more conviction than any sermons, apologetics, or books on piety.

Such love is only possible as God pours out His love on us. "We love because he first loved us" (1 John 4:19). As we experience His love, we are enabled through Him to love others as ourselves. If the church lived like this then the world would believe.

17
How to Find Life
Matthew 7:13–14

13 Enter through the narrow gate. For wide is the gate and broad is the road that leads to destruction, and many enter through it. 14 But small is the gate and narrow the road that leads to life, and only a few find it.

There comes a point in all our lives when we have to reach a decision. I practiced as a lawyer for a number of years, and one of the first cases in which I was involved was a long and complicated fraud case, involving commodity options. The four defendants had taken large quantities of money from people and were unable to repay them. After six months the jury retired to consider their verdict. They deliberated for a week and when they returned to court they were asked, in the usual way, this question: "Have you reached a verdict on which you are all agreed?"

Throughout the Sermon on the Mount, Jesus spent some time explaining to the people what it means to be a Christian—the kind of character, lifestyle, secret life, relationships, and attitudes we need to have. Now, as He comes to the end of the sermon, He says that it is decision time. It is time to reach a verdict.

One of the biggest decisions many of us face in our lives is who we are going to marry. A great deal hangs on the decision. In September, 1977, at the age of 22, I was having dinner with Pippa in a farmhouse in the Dordogne in central France. It was a beautiful evening with a stunning sunset. I had planned to ask her to marry me, but I was worried that she would say 'no.' So I did not ask her straight out. Instead I asked first: "Would you ever like to get married?" She did not have too much trouble with the first question.

195

She said, "Yes." So I embarked on the second: "Whom would you most like to marry?" Quick as a flash she replied, "Prince Charles." With great diffidence I finally plucked up the courage and asked, "Would you marry me?" At that moment she made a decision that was going to affect the whole course of the rest of our lives. Thankfully, she said, "Yes."

Jesus, in this passage, is asking us to make an even bigger decision. As Michael Green has said, the Sermon on the Mount is not just "a collection of ethical maxims such as might have been devised by any cultivated humanist." [122] There is a call to decide about the person of Jesus Christ. We have to reach a verdict. The decision we make, Jesus tells us, will affect not only the rest of our lives, but the whole of eternity. Jesus says that ultimately there are only two alternatives—to follow Him or not to follow Him; to be a Christian, or not to be a Christian.

WHAT IS THE DIFFERENCE?

Jesus lays before us two possible lifestyles and answers the question: "Is it going to be easy?" He says there are two roads, one is "broad" (vs. 13) and one is "narrow" (vs. 14).

The Greek word for the former means "broad, spacious, roomy." There are no boundaries and you can do what you like. You don't have to give up anything; tolerance and permissiveness are the order of the day. You can live a life of ease, without having to keep to the standards Jesus has just set out in the Sermon on the Mount. You can be proud and angry, you can hate your enemy and be full of lust. You need not forgive and you need never pray or fast. You can hold on to all your money and you can be ambitious for yourself. If someone does you wrong, you can retaliate as much as you like and criticize others to your heart's content.

The problem with this road, of course, is that where there are no boundaries people get hurt. We all recognize that children need boundaries or else they end up as spoiled brats, but what we some-times forget is that adults can be spoiled brats too, and that is even more obnoxious. Further, the result of life on the broad road is that other people get hurt. My freedom to "drive dangerously" means that someone else may get injured or killed. My freedom to be lustful means someone else is abused. If I feel at liberty to steal, then some-one else gets robbed. My freedom to get divorced means that my children come from a broken home.

The other road is "narrow" (vs.14). This word means "restricted, confined, compressed." This is the pressurized road and there are boundaries. Humility is the order of the day. It is a road where there is no unrighteous anger allowed, no lust, no swearing, no retaliation, and no hatred. You have to give, to pray, to fast, to seek first the kingdom of God. It is a road of purity, honesty, and forgiveness. It is a road where we are required to "do to others what you would have them do to you" (Matthew 7:12). Life is much more difficult, especially as you can expect that people will "falsely say all kinds of evil against you because of me [Jesus]" (Matthew 5:11).

Not only is it a more difficult road, it is virtually impossible to keep Jesus' standards. It is certainly impossible to keep them without Him. But on this road Jesus goes with us and that is what makes it a much more exciting path. We do not walk alone.

During the winter, I have the privilege of doing a two-week chaplaincy in a ski resort. On one occasion we were joined by Emmy Wilson, who had been a representative of the Ski Club of Great Britain, a qualified ski guide, and hence is a brilliant and graceful skier. I had been skiing on nice, flat blue runs, but suddenly she was taking us down narrow, steep black runs, full of moguls and in blizzard conditions. It was certainly the best skiing of my life and it was exhilarating, challenging, and exciting. I would have hated it on my own, but somehow I felt safe skiing with Emmy, as she knew what she was doing.

The Christian life is an exciting adventure. G. K. Chesterton described it as the "whirling adventure of Christ." Dorothy Sayers spoke of the "careless rage for life." Jim Elliott, the missionary, spoke of "reckless abandonment." The founder of the Salvation Army, William Booth, described Christians as "godly, go-ahead dare devils."

WHERE DO THEY LEAD?

Secondly, Jesus sets before us two possible destinations and answers the question: "Where am I heading?" The broad road with its wide entrance, He warns us, leads ultimately to "destruction" (vs. 13), whereas the narrow road with its narrow gate "leads to life" (vs. 14).

I remember reading years ago of an incident in the Italian Riviera. A young man was driving his sports car along a road near the sea. All along the road were warning signs that the road was not yet completed and that no one should be on that road, but he continued at great speed, went over the cliff, and killed himself.

Jesus warns us here that the life on the broad road, which might seem quite harmless, actually leads to destruction. Pride, anger, lust, hatred, greed, unforgiveness, selfishness, and all the other things which Jesus has been speaking about will eventually destroy us, as well as others.

One of the world's most famous paintings is "The Last Supper" by Leonardo Da Vinci. It took him four years to paint it. It is said that when he began, he looked for a man to model for Jesus. He wanted to find someone whose face was full of love and had expressions worthy of Jesus. Not surprisingly he had a hard task! Eventually he found a man called Pietro Bandinelli who sat for him. Four years later he looked for a man to model Judas, the last of the disciples to be painted. He went out onto the streets and searched for a man whose face showed appropriate suspicion, anger, and bitterness. He found such a man. When he finished painting him he asked his name. "Pietro Bandinelli," was the reply. Four years down the line, sin had

had a destructive effect on that man, who no longer even looked the same. So with us, the addictive power of sin will destroy us.

Sometimes we can see sin in others, but we find it much harder to see it in ourselves because we live with it and it grows gradually in us. About nine years ago, my wife and I bought a second-hand car, which was then only 18 months old. It was bright and shining and we were even embarrassed about how nice it looked. However, it was soon involved in one or two minor scrapes. Among other things I backed it into a tree. In all the nine years I don't think we ever washed it once, so gradually rust began to develop. But we never really noticed. Then, we sold the car and recently I saw it again. I was so shocked. I had never understood why people laughed when they looked at it. When I saw it this time I could see why. It was a complete wreck.

Jesus warns us that the broad road lifestyle will destroy us. As an image of this, Jesus sometimes used the word "Gehenna," which was the trash dump in the valley of Hinnem outside Jerusalem. This trash dump was a nasty place, where the slow fire burned ceaselessly and the worms steadily consumed the rotting rubbish. This is not a threat, but rather it is a warning.

Jesus warns us about where the broad road leads. God loves us and in His love He puts up warning sign after warning sign. He has given us consciences and He has put a hunger in our hearts which can only be satisfied by a relationship with Him through His Son, Jesus Christ. He gives us opportunities through other Christians. Anyone reading this chapter in the Bible is reading a warning sign.

On the other hand, Jesus tells us that the narrow road, with its narrow gate, leads to life. There are two Greek words for life. One means "earthly, biological life." The other, which is used here, means both "life in the physical sense" and "the supernatural life belonging to God and Christ, which the believers will receive in the future, but which they also enjoy here and now." [123] This eternal life is only made possible because Jesus died on the cross for us so that we might know

God. Jesus defines eternal life like this: "Now this is eternal life: that they may know you, the only true God, and Jesus Christ, whom you have sent" (John 17:3).

If we simply compared the two roads, we might easily make the wrong decision. The psalmist speaks of how he looked at those who, in effect, were on the broad road and became envious of them. They appeared to have no struggles, they were prosperous, and they had strong, healthy bodies. They seemed free from the usual burdens of life. He thought: "In vain have I kept my heart pure . . . till I entered the sanctuary of God; then I understood their final destiny" (Psalm 73:13, 17).

Mother Teresa started an order which now has 537 houses throughout the world in 137 countries. They help house lepers, the dying, the mentally ill, people with tuberculosis, and children. Before she died, she gave an interview to *Hello!* magazine and the final questions went like this:

When you think of how much you have achieved in the last 50 years, Mother, you must surely feel just a little bit pleased with yourself?
It is not my achievement. I am not important, it is the work that's important. God has helped us and the money has kept coming. I don't think in terms of achievement, I just think about what needs to be done for the sick and the poor. I really don't have any time to be pleased with myself.

And how is your health these days? Reportedly you've had a chesty cough for several weeks which you can't shake off.
I don't have any time to think about my health either. This cough I have is a gift from God, a birthday present!

When Pope John Paul II visited you here, you said it was the happiest day of your life. What moved you so much about that occasion?
When he arrived in Calcutta he didn't come here but went straight to the Home for the Dying. That was his priority. After that, whenever we met in Rome I would say to him, "You have so much space in front of the Vatican, Holy Father. Why don't you give me a house for all these people in your

city who need help?" I think it was on my third visit that he handed me a set of keys. It was for a home in Rome. Here we give shelter to 85 women who were forced into prostitution as their only means of survival.

What do you say to people who think you should attack the social causes of poverty as well as alleviate its suffering?
This work has no connection with politics. Our duty is to serve the poor whatever way we can, and what they desperately need is food, clothes, and medicines. We have no time for politics. There are so many things that we need to do here and so little time to do them in.

You've recently celebrated your eighty-fourth birthday. Are you at all afraid of dying?
How can I be, when I have watched and been with so many who have died? Dying is going home to God. You come from there and you go back there. I've never been afraid. No, on the contrary, I look forward to it. [124]

WHO IS ON THE ROADS?

Thirdly, Jesus sets before us two groups of people and answers the question: "Who will go with me?" There are "many" (vs.13) on the broad road, with its wide entrance, although it leads to destruction. However, on the narrow road, although it leads to life, there are only a few people.

The large crowd on the broad road can give people a false sense of security. "Everybody else on the road can't be wrong," we think. But they can. As G. K. Chesterton put it: "Right is right, even if nobody does it. Wrong is wrong, even if everybody is wrong about it."

A team of doctors decided to conduct an experiment to study the ways in which group pressure influences young people. Ten teenagers were invited into a room, apparently to assess their eyesight.

Three cards were to be held up, each with a line on it. The students were told to raise their hands when the longest line was shown. One student, however, was unaware that the other nine had been instructed to vote for the second longest line.

201

When his nine companions voted incorrectly, despite their obvious mistake, he voted with them. When the experiment was repeated, again and again he voted with the group, even though he knew they were wrong.

As the psychologist James Dobson commented:

> This one young man was not unusual. *More than 75% of young people tested behaved that same way. They sat there time after time, saying a short line was longer than a long line!* They simply didn't have the courage to say, "The group is wrong. I can't explain why, but you guys are all confused." A small percentage—only 25 out of 100—had the courage to take their stand against the group, even when the majority was obviously wrong. [125]

Sometimes we have to stand alone. Recently I heard about Mr. Gugi Hara, who worked in the Embassy in Japan during the war. When everyone was refusing visas to the Jews and no country was willing to take them, he issued 6,000–10,000 visas. In that way he saved many lives. After the war he was forced to take early retirement and he died eight years ago, unknown and unrecognized. Now, 50 years after the event, as Japan reassesses the war, he is regarded as a hero.

Jesus contrasts the "many" on the broad road with the "few" on the narrow road. The few are not as few as all that. John speaks in Revelation of "a great multitude that no one could count, from every nation, tribe, people and language." (Revelation 7:9). There are estimated to be 1.7 billion Christians in the world today. That is a considerable number, even though it is only a minority of the world's total population.

As members of a minority, we can often feel alone. We may be the only Christian in our work place, or the only Christian among our family, or in the neighborhood. That is not a reason to stay on the broad road; rather, it is a reason to get off quickly. In doing so we may encourage others to follow.

When Charles Finney was preaching at Rochester, New York, in the 1830s, a great many lawyers came to hear him. One night, way up in the gallery sat the Chief Justice of the Court of Appeals for the State of New York. As he listened to Finney's proclamation of the Gospel he became convinced of the truth of it. Then the question came to him: "Will you go forward like the other ordinary men and women?" Something in him said that it would never do, because of his prestigious social position (at the top of the legal hierarchy of New York State). He sat there thinking for a while, then he said to himself, "Why not? I am convinced of the truth. . . . I know my duty; why should I not do it like any other person?" He got up from his place in the gallery, went down the stairway, and came up the stairs at the back to where Finney was preaching. Finney, in the middle of his sermon, felt someone tugging at his jacket. He turned around and saw the Chief Justice. He asked, "What is it?"

The Chief Justice replied, "Mr. Finney, if you will call people forward I will come."

Finney stopped his sermon and said, "The Chief Justice says that if I call people forward he will come. I ask you to come forward now." The Chief Justice went forward and almost every lawyer in Rochester was converted. It is said that 100,000 people were converted in 12 months in that area.

We may not be able to have quite that effect, but we may be able to help someone on to the right road.

HOW DO I GET IN?

Fourthly, Jesus lays before us two entrances and answers the question: "How do I get in?" One entrance is "wide" (vs. 13); the other is "small" (vs. 14).

On the broad road there is easy access through a wide gate. There are many ways in which you can enter. You could be an atheist, an agnostic, a New Ager, or a mixture of all of them. On the other hand, the entrance to the narrow road is itself a narrow one. There is only one way in, and that is by repentance and faith in Jesus Christ. You cannot take sin in with you and you have to turn your back on everything you know to be wrong. That is not at all easy. The longer you have been on the wrong road, the harder it is to admit, and to change, although it is never too late to do so.

Bernard Levin wrote an article about a man named Andrew Rothstein who had recently died at the age of 95. He was one of those whose "gods" were Lenin and Stalin. Bernard Levin wrote as follows:

> When did Andrew Rothstein fail as a human being? More to the point, why did he never wish to be a full human being? I have met many who repented, and when asking that question I found that for many of them it was a kind of inertia, but a very singular kind. Again and again, when I have asked the question "Why did you not break away, but continue living a lie and knowing it to be a lie?" and the answer is profoundly painful for the repentant, and indeed for me. The answer is: "We had gone on so far, we realized that if we stopped now, our lives would have been worthless." [126]

On the narrow road access is hard because the gate is "small." We can only enter by faith in Jesus Christ. We live in an age of pluralism, and the suggestion that there is only one way to God is not popular to the modern ear, but that is the claim of Jesus Christ. We have to decide what to make of it, and reach a verdict.

At the beginning of this chapter, I mentioned a court case in which I was involved and that the jury were asked the question: "Have you reached a verdict on which you are all agreed?" They had to reply that they were not agreed and could not decide. That is not an option open to us. Everyone is on one of the two roads. It is an uncomfortable fact that there is no middle road, no third gate, no neutral group. If we are on the broad road we do not need to do anything in order to stay on it. But if we want to get off it we need to enter the narrow gate through repentance and faith in Jesus Christ. As we enter through the narrow gate, we find that although there may not be huge numbers on the road, we are not alone. Jesus Christ Himself goes with us.

18
How to Discern False Prophets

Matthew 7:15–23

15 Watch out for false prophets. They come to you in sheep's clothing, but inwardly they are ferocious wolves. 16 By their fruit you will recognize them. Do people pick grapes from thornbushes, or figs from thistles? 17 Likewise every good tree bears good fruit, but a bad tree bears bad fruit. 18 A good tree cannot bear bad fruit, and a bad tree cannot bear good fruit. 19 Every tree that does not bear good fruit is cut down and thrown into the fire. 20 Thus, by their fruit you will recognize them.

21 Not everyone who says to me, "Lord, Lord," will enter the kingdom of heaven, but only he who does the will of my Father who is in heaven. 22 Many will say to me on that day, "Lord, Lord, did we not prophesy in your name, and in your name drive out demons and perform many miracles?" 23 Then I will tell them plainly, "I never knew you. Away from me, you evildoers!"

Inside lay 18 bodies—men, women and a boy about ten years old—arrayed in a crude circle, feet toward the center. Many wore red-and-black or white-and-gold ceremonial robes, some with their hands tied behind their backs. Most had been shot in the head or neck; ten had plastic bags over their heads. Empty champagne bottles littered the floor; on the wall hung a painting of a Christ-like figure with a rose above his head. Another corpse turned up in a room off to the side. In an adjoining circular chapel, police uncovered three additional bodies and a jarring collection of clues: an altar with a rose and a cross and a golden chalice. [127]

News reports, such as this one from Switzerland, spectacularly highlight the disastrous results of the false teaching of a cult.

In November 1978, 913 people died in a mass suicide in Jonestown, Guyana. Of these, 200 were children and another 200 were over the age of 65. Babies had cyanide squirted into their mouths, while adults lined up to drink theirs. More recently, in Waco, Texas, 87 deaths followed an assault by the FBI on the Branch Davidian sect led by David Koresh. One recent survey estimated there to be 1,317 cults in Europe and 425 in the United States.

In the earlier part of the Sermon on the Mount, Jesus warned against attacks from outside the church in the form of persecution. Now He adds a solemn warning about attacks which come from the inside. He tells us that we are to "watch out for false prophets" (vs. 15). This kind of language is foreign to modern thinking, so it is helpful to be more specific. There are those kinds of false prophets, as in the examples above, who are clearly outside the community of orthodox Christian belief, but who claim nonetheless to be the true (and the only) people of God. However, there are others who speak from within the church, and who appear to be saying godly things, but in reality are leading people away from God. Some in the church may say: "Surely all spiritual teachers are good" or, "Surely, if a person talks about God and heals people, it must be all right." But Jesus tells us that this is not the case. There is a need to discern. In spite of the contemporary love of choosing to hold incompatible beliefs together, there is a distinction between true and false, and we need to discern the difference.

The word "prophet" here includes anyone who speaks "in the name of the Lord." False prophets include not only those who claim to have a prophetic ministry in the narrow sense, but also anyone who claims to speak from God, such as pastors, priests, Christian teachers, evangelists, and preachers. In all these cases, we need to distinguish the true from the false.

Jesus gives us a very serious warning about false prophets. He says that they are "ferocious wolves" (vs. 15). The wolf is the natural enemy of the sheep. The same description is used elsewhere in the Bible to describe officials, rulers, governors, and false teachers who are enemies of God's people (Ezekiel 22:27; Zephaniah 3:3; Matthew 10:16; John 10:12; Acts 20:29). It is a very serious matter to harm God's people and Jesus warns that such people will be like trees that are "cut down and thrown into the fire" (vs. 19). On the Day of Judgment He will say to them, "Away from me, you evildoers!" (vs. 23). John Wesley emphasizes the seriousness of the matter by declaring that such people "murder the souls of men."

How are we to spot these false teachers? Jesus tells us about the test which will not reveal them, and also about the one test which will.

THE WRONG TEST: LOOKING ON THE OUTSIDE

The wrong test is a superficial one. It looks only at the outward clothing. This does not work because "ferocious wolves" can appear "in sheep's clothing" (vs. 15). "Sheep's clothing" could include an outward profession of faith. Jesus says, "Not everyone who says to me, 'Lord, Lord,' will enter the kingdom of heaven, but only he who does the will of my Father who is in heaven" (vs. 21). Verbal profession is not enough. It is not sufficient to know all the Christian jargon and recite the Christian creeds.

The "sheep's clothing" could also include supernatural activity. Jesus warns that "many will say to me on that day, 'Lord, Lord, did we not prophesy in your name, and in your name drive out demons and perform many miracles?' Then I will tell them plainly, 'I never knew you. Away from me, you evildoers!' " (vss. 22–23). It is interesting to note in passing that Jesus is not speaking against the activities themselves. He clearly expected that his people would "prophesy," "drive out demons," and "perform miracles." Indeed, Matthew's inclusion of this passage suggests that these activities were continuing in the church. [128] Yet in themselves they are not sufficient to prove that a prophet is genuine.

THE RIGHT TEST: LOOKING ON THE INSIDE

There is only one true test which Jesus gives, and He repeats it: "By their fruit you will recognize them" (vss. 16, 20). Jesus does not say that you will know them by their roots. Some have suggested that a work of God should be tested by its roots—i.e., who has been involved at an earlier stage. This is not the test Jesus gives. It would be an impossible one to apply. The whole point about roots is that they are underground. It would often take years to investigate a person's roots. Fruit, on the other hand, is visible and is relatively easy to test. Jesus explains the test more fully: "Do people pick grapes from thornbushes, or figs from thistles? Likewise every good tree bears good fruit, but a bad tree bears bad fruit. A good tree cannot bear bad fruit, and a bad tree cannot bear good fruit. Every tree that does not bear good fruit is cut down and thrown into the fire" (vss. 16–19).

In the Middle East there was a thornbush which, at a distance, looked very like a vine. It had little black berries which closely resembled grapes. There was also a thistle which produced a flower which could be mistaken for a fig. On closer inspection it would be revealed that the thornbush did not produce grapes and the thistle did not produce figs. As John Stott puts it, "Noxious weeds like thorns and thistles cannot produce edible fruit like grapes and figs." [129] Nor can a diseased tree produce good fruit, whereas a tree that is in good condition will produce good fruit.

One result of this is that although we are to be wise and

discerning, we are not to be suspicious of everyone, and neither are we to become heresy hunters, for false prophets will reveal themselves by their fruit. We need not worry.

What is the fruit we should look at? It will involve at least six aspects.

The fruit of character: who they are

The image of fruit is picked up by Paul in his classic description of Christian character: "The fruit of the Spirit is love, joy, peace, patience, kindness, goodness, faithfulness, gentleness and self-control. Against such things there is no law" (Galatians 5:22–23). These are the characteristics we expect to see growing in a person who is a true Christian and has the Holy Spirit of God living within.

We have already seen that Jesus started the Sermon on the Mount with precisely this issue of character. A true follower of Jesus Christ will begin to develop the kind of character described in Matthew 5:1–16. There should be humility, a thirst for righteousness, a merciful attitude, meekness, purity, and all the other characteristics described in that passage.

We need especially to look at Christian leaders and ask questions about their character. Of course, we will never find perfection, as all leaders are still human beings and subject to the same temptations and weaknesses as the rest of us. But we need to ask whether there are fundamental flaws in their characters.

For example, with many cult leaders there is a disturbing arrogance, which should put us on our guard. We should always be suspicious of those who, in their arrogance, exclude all others. Many cults regard themselves as the only real Christians in the world. I remember asking one cult member, "How many Christians are there in Spain?" The answer was "none" because that particular cult did not operate in Spain. It did not matter as far as they were concerned whether they were Roman Catholic, Anglican, Methodist,

Baptist, Pentecostal, or any other denomination, as his cult considered none of them to be genuine. A doctor writing about the cults in *The Big Issue* wrote:

> I myself met David Icke, and others of the many prophets claiming to be on a mission from God, on a TV program . . . and was asked to diagnose his mental illness . . . he was entirely sane in the medical sense. Such people do not hear voices or genuinely believe they are God. What they suffer from is megalomania, self-centeredness and a sophisticated ability to manipulate the vulnerable. [130]

The type of conduct: what they do

Jesus says that those who enter the kingdom of heaven will be those who do the will of His Father (vs. 21). To the wolves He says, "Away from me, you evildoers!" (vs. 23).

What we believe will affect how we live. Our creed determines our conduct. We need to look at leaders and see how their lives match up to Jesus' teaching in the Sermon on the Mount in terms of righteous living, anger, lust, integrity, and loving our enemies.

When we look at the cults, we so often see, for example, great sexual immorality. Both Jim Jones (Jonestown) and David Koresh (Waco) plucked sexual partners at will from their flocks. Koresh even persuaded his followers that because his seed was divine, only he had the right to procreate. "The Children of God," sometimes known as "the Family of Love," led by David Berg, used to recruit through what they called "flirty fishing" (sexual seduction) and indulge in group promiscuity.

The content of their teaching: what they say

Later on in Matthew's Gospel Jesus uses a similar image of fruitfulness in relation to what people say:

> Make a tree good and its fruit will be good, or make a tree bad and its fruit will be bad, for a tree is recognized by its fruit. You brood of vipers, how

211

can you who are evil say anything good? For out of the overflow of the heart the mouth speaks. The good man brings good things out of the good stored up in him, and the evil man brings evil things out of the evil stored up in him. But I tell you that men will have to give account on the day of judgment for every careless word they have spoken. For by your words you will be acquitted, and by your words you will be condemned (Matthew 12:33–37).

One of the Old Testament tests of the true prophet came in Deuteronomy 13. Even if a prophet performed signs and wonders, if he said, "Let us follow other gods," the people were warned, "You must not listen to the words of that prophet" (Deuteronomy 13:1–3). In other words, the people were to test the prophet by his teaching—whether he led people to God or away from Him.

We need to weigh the words of anyone who claims to speak on behalf of God against what we know to be the Word of God. How do the words of the prophet stand up against the teaching of Scripture? We need to follow the example of the Bereans who "received the message with great eagerness and examined the Scriptures every day to see if what Paul said was true" (Acts 17:11).

Cults and sects often claim that the authority of the Bible is not enough for us and rely also on some other source of authority. The Church of the Latter Day Saints invoke as their authority the Bible and the Book of Mormon; Christian Scientists look to the Bible and Mary Baker Eddy; Jehovah's Witnesses have their own version of the Bible. In addition, they always depart from at least one major historic doctrine of the Christian faith, such as the Trinity, or the divinity of Christ.

The style of their relationships: how they love
Love for other Christians is the command of Jesus. If we obey this command, we will remain in the vine and bear fruit. Love and fruitfulness go hand in hand (John 15:10–12). Indeed, as we have seen, love is the first fruit of the Spirit that Paul mentions in

Galatians 5:22.

Jesus' warning to watch out for "false prophets" needs to be set alongside his admonition in the previous section: "Do not judge, or you too will be judged" (Matthew 7:1).

There is a delicate balance. We need to beware of judging and condemning other Christians—of spotting the speck of sawdust in their eyes and missing the major blind spot in our own. Some are far too quick to write off other Christians. Harsh judgmentalism combined with exclusiveness is one of the marks of cults. Sadly, it is also sometimes seen within the Christian church where believers can be too quick to judge and condemn other genuine Christians.

The results of their influence: the effect they have
We need to ask what the fruit of the ministry is, in terms of the effect it has on the lives of the congregation. Is it producing a congregation united in love, full of joy, living at peace, full of kindness to others, doing good, and showing themselves to be faithful, gentle, and self-controlled? Is it producing the sort of people and lifestyle Jesus has commanded through this sermon?

The test of preaching is what effect it has on people. Of course, we cannot judge by a single, possibly unrepresentative, member of the congregation. But if we look at the congregation as a whole we will get some feel of the effect.

Jesus told us, "A student is not above his teacher, but everyone who is fully trained will be like his teacher" (Luke 6:40). The main question to ask about the sermons is not, "Are they intellectually stimulating?" or, "Are the stories funny and the headings memorable?" Rather, we should be asking, "Are they bringing the people closer to God?'

The depth of their relationship with Jesus: who they are in private
In John 15, Jesus uses the image of the vine. Jesus is the vine and we are the branches. If we stay close to Jesus we will bear much fruit, but

without Him we can do nothing. The way to produce fruit is to be personally and vitally related to Jesus. Unless we are in this relationship we will bear no fruit. Jesus says, "Apart from me you can do nothing" (John 15:5). Hence, Jesus will say to the false prophets on the last day, "I never knew you" (vs. 23). They were not living in a relationship with Jesus Christ, and the unseen roots of secret giving, private prayer, and private fasting had not been built up.

Jeremiah warns against the false prophets who have visions from their own mind, and not from the mouth of the Lord. This is one of the Old Testament tests of a true prophet. He asks, "But which of them has stood in the council of the LORD to see or to hear his word?" (Jeremiah 23:18).

The true prophet knows Jesus Christ, listens to Him and speaks His word. God has given us His Word and His Spirit to enable us to test whether a prophet is genuinely from Him.

19
How to Build a Secure Future

Matthew 7:24–29

²⁴ *"Therefore everyone who hears these words of mine and puts them into practice is like a wise man who built his house on the rock.* ²⁵ *The rain came down, the streams rose, and the winds blew and beat against that house; yet it did not fall, because it had its foundation on the rock.* ²⁶ *But everyone who hears these words of mine and does not put them into practice is like a foolish man who built his house on sand.* ²⁷ *The rain came down, the streams rose, and the winds blew and beat against that house, and it fell with a great crash."*

²⁸ *When Jesus had finished saying these things, the crowds were amazed at his teaching,* ²⁹ *because he taught as one who had authority, and not as their teachers of the law.*

There is a big difference between hearing and doing. Some years ago, I decided I would like to take up windsurfing. It looked fun, and relatively easy to learn. I bought a book all about it and learned the theory. We went on a vacation by the sea and I rented a board for an hour. It was a hot day, so I covered myself in sun oil. The first time I fell in, the sun oil came off me and onto the board. Thereafter, I fell first forward and then backward, time and again. Soon word spread around the beach that something amusing was occurring and a crowd gathered and began to cheer. I learned that there is a great difference between hearing about how to windsurf and actually doing it.

The last three sections of the Sermon on the Mount are all about decisions. Which gate will we enter: the broad or the narrow? Whom will we follow: the true or the false prophet? Now, finally, Jesus requires us to decide on what we will base our lives: on rock or on sand. Once again, Jesus presents us with only two alternatives. In the current climate of pluralism and permissiveness we would like to think that there are many different ways to build our lives. Yet Jesus tells us here that there are ultimately only two alternatives. In the previous section He contrasted "doing" and "saying," but in this one he contrasts "doing" and "hearing." He tells us about two men, two houses, two foundations, two results, and two responses to Jesus.

SUPERFICIAL SIMILARITIES

Both the wise man and the foolish man "built his house" (vss. 24, 26). Jesus knew all about building houses. He was a craftsman by trade and had practiced as a carpenter. The illustration He uses is the down-to-earth one of a practical man. Two men both decided to build a house. No doubt they intended to live in and enjoy them, perhaps with their families. Both were building something of long-lasting significance. The houses they built differed little in appearance. At this stage no one looking on from outside, in a purely superficial way, would have been able to tell them apart.

The second similarity between the two is that in both cases "the rain came down, the streams rose, and the winds blew and beat against that house" (vss. 25, 27). All of us, sooner or later, face inevitable pressures of life in this world. These include suffering, sickness, bereavement, disappointment and misunderstandings, trials and temptations, doubts and satanic attacks. Ultimately, all of us will face death and God's judgment. The image of "rain ... torrents ... winds" is used in Ezekiel to refer to God's judgment (Ezekiel 13:11), but the language of judgment is not confined to the Old Testament. As C. S. Lewis pointed out, "All the most terrifying texts came from the mouth of our Lord."[131] Jesus here and elsewhere warns of the coming judgment, as do the other New Testament writers.

216

Thirdly, both people had the opportunity to respond. Jesus says that both the wise and the foolish hear "these words of mine" (vss. 24, 26). Today, many people hear the words of Jesus. They are taught in Sunday school lessons, and millions of people have their own Bibles. Many have been to churches or meetings, or heard an evangelist like Billy Graham. They may have been baptized and confirmed. However, Jesus says that hearing His words is not enough.

UNDERLYING DIFFERENCES

Although there are superficial similarities, the underlying differences are so great that Jesus can describe one of the builders as "a wise man" (vs. 24), whereas the other is "a foolish man" (vs. 26). Literally, the word means "moron" or "idiot." Why does Jesus use such strong language? The second underlying difference gives us the answer.

The difference is in the foundations. The wise man built "on the rock" (vs. 24), whereas the foolish man built "on sand" (vs. 26). It is not entirely clear whether in this version of the parable Jesus is speaking of a difference in location or a difference in depth. In Matthew's version, it could be a difference in location. The wise man goes on looking until he finds rock on which to build, whereas the foolish man "chooses an attractive stretch of sand, not realizing that it is a dry *wadi* which in winter will become a raging torrent."[132] Or it could be that the fool builds on sand, but the wise man digs until he finds the rock beneath it. Certainly, in Luke's version of the parable, Jesus speaks of a man "building a house, who dug down deep and laid the foundation on rock" (Luke 6:48), as opposed to the man who "built a house on the ground without a foundation" (Luke 6:49).

The foolish man, possibly in a hurry, does not stop and ask the farsighted questions of life. He takes a short-term view and does not think ahead. Indeed, he hardly seems to think at all. The wise man goes to a great deal more trouble, thinking and planning for the long term. A foolish person only thinks about immediate gratification from money, sex, power, or relationships. It is foolish to go through life without thinking about the foundational questions regarding the meaning of life. Unless we answer the questions of why we are here and what the point of life is, we will never know whether our plans are right or wrong, good or bad. If we don't know what life is for, we'll use it wrongly. Bishop Lesslie Newbigin tells the story of when he was a schoolboy:

> There was a great Boy Scout Jamboree in Liverpool and about the same time a new substance had been unleashed on the world said to be edible and called "Shredded Wheat." On one day of the camp this Shredded Wheat was issued as rations for all the troops and at 10:00 there was a complaint in the camp office from the scouts assigned to clean-up, "These pan-scrubbers are no use!"

218

"These shredded wheats are tough"

The third underlying difference is that because the foundations of their houses (which represent our lives) are so different, the results are equally different. When "the rain came down, the streams rose, and the winds blew and beat against that house" (vss. 25, 27), the house built on the rock "did not fall" (vs. 25), but the other one "fell with a great crash" (vs. 27). These are solemn words of warning. As John Calvin put it, "True piety is not fully distinguished from its counterfeit till it comes to the trial."[133] The trial may be during this life or it may come on the Day of Judgment. What is certain, according to Jesus, is that it will come.

Again, this is not a threat, but a warning from Jesus. He warned of the danger of "destruction" (vs. 13), of the "fire" (vs. 19), of being told, "Away from me, you evildoers!" (vs. 23), and now He warns of a "great crash" (vs. 27). Jesus knew that in the long run it is more loving to warn people by telling them the truth. On Wednesday, March 13, 1991, there was a disaster on the M4 motorway, one of Britain's busiest freeways. Ten people died and 25 people were injured on a foggy day in one of Britain's worst road accidents. One man, named Alan Bateman, was hailed as a hero after he climbed out of his damaged car and ran along the shoulder to try to warn oncoming vehicles of the wreckage ahead. Some drivers sounded their horns at him, however, and drove on toward the crash.

Jesus warns us, not in order to frighten us, but because He loves us and wants us to avoid the crash. He wants us to be like the wise man whose house "did not fall" (vs. 25), but stood the test. The promise of Jesus is that a house built on the rock will withstand the storms of life. A life founded on obedience to Jesus is safe, no matter what the storms of life may bring. The 19th-century evangelist, D. L. Moody, wrote in his Bible alongside this verse, "Build on the rock and fear no shock."

The apostle Paul testified to how this was true in his own life. He did not avoid life's problems. He wrote to a church which was questioning his qualifications for Christian leadership:

> I have worked much harder, been in prison more frequently, been flogged more severely, and been exposed to death again and again. Five times I received from the Jews the forty lashes minus one. Three times I was beaten with rods, once I was stoned, three times I was shipwrecked, I spent a night and a day in the open sea, I have been constantly on the move. I have been in danger from rivers, in danger from bandits, in danger from my own countrymen, in danger from Gentiles; in danger in the city, in danger in the country, in danger at sea; and in danger from false brothers. I have labored and toiled and have often gone without sleep; I have known hunger and thirst and have often gone without food; I have been cold and naked. Besides everything else, I face daily the pressure of my concern for all the churches (2 Corinthians 11:23–28).

Amazingly, Paul could also write, "Our light and momentary troubles are achieving for us an eternal glory that far outweighs them all. So we fix our eyes not on what is seen, but on what is unseen. For what is seen is temporary, but what is unseen is eternal" (2 Corinthians 4:17–18). Paul knew that, as Jesus had promised, a life built on Him would stand not only in this life, but for all eternity. The wise man takes the long view.

The coming storms refer not only to the trials of this life, but also to the ultimate trial of the Day of Judgment. The wise man looks forward to "a new heaven and a new earth" (Revelation 21:1). He will spend eternity in the presence of Jesus (Revelation 21:3). He knows that on that day he will receive a glorious resurrection body and that, as Jesus rose from the dead as the "first fruits" (1 Corinthians 15), he will experience intense joy which goes on forever. "No eye has seen, no ear has heard, no mind has conceived what God has prepared for those who love him" (1 Corinthians 2:9).

Even in this life we get glimpses of this joy. The Holy Spirit has been given to us as a down payment, guaranteeing what is to come (Ephesians 1:13–14). It is not just a guarantee; we actually begin to experience some of the joys of heaven here and now.

THE KEY DIFFERENCE

Jesus tells us that the key difference is that the wise man not only hears the words of Jesus, he "puts them into practice" (vs. 24). The foolish man, on the other hand, although he hears His words "does not put them into practice" (vs. 26). We need to be clear that Jesus is not saying that we earn our way into the kingdom of God by good works. This would be contrary to what Jesus says elsewhere in the Sermon on the Mount. It is those who recognize their poverty of spirit to whom the kingdom of God belongs (Matthew 5:3). The rest of the New Testament underlines this and, in the book of Romans, Paul expounds why no one can be justified by their own works, but only by grace through faith in Christ.

Secondly, Jesus does not mean that a person who puts His "words into practice" leads a sinless life. Paul summarizes his argument in the first three chapters of Romans thus: "All have sinned and fall short of the glory of God" (Romans 3:23). John tells us, "If we claim to be without sin, we deceive ourselves and the truth is not in us" (1 John 1:8).

If, then, Jesus is not teaching justification by works or sinless perfection, what is He teaching here? He is teaching what He taught elsewhere and what the rest of the New Testament affirms, that listening alone is not enough. Hearing must lead to action (see also Romans 2:13; James. 1:22–25; 2:14–20; 1 John 1:6; 2:4). As in Jesus' day, the theological and religious world today is full of hearing. It is, as Michael Green puts it, "overloaded with God-talk."[134] But college courses on the Bible, or even a degree in theology, is not enough. Knowledge must lead to action, theory must be put into practice, our theology must affect our lives—or else we are building our lives on sand.

To put the words of Jesus into practice will first mean repentance. The Sermon on the Mount has been described as "a terrifying call to repentance."[135] As we look at the standards set in the sermon we see how desperately far short we all fall. We cry out to God for mercy and turn our backs on the old life. We repent of our lack of love, unforgiveness, anger, lust, and pride.

Secondly, it means putting our faith in Jesus. As we see how far short of His standards we fall, we recognize we cannot save ourselves and we desperately need a Savior. The name Jesus means "savior." Matthew tells us earlier in his Gospel that the angel of the Lord told Joseph, His father, "You are to give him the name Jesus, because he will save his people from their sins" (Matthew 1:21). Jesus alone can save us. That is why He came to earth to die on the cross and rise again—so that we could be forgiven and set free. He came "to give his life as a ransom for many" (Mark 10:45).

Thirdly, we recognize that we cannot possibly live up to the standards of the Sermon on the Mount without help from outside. They are unattainable and we need the power of the Holy Spirit in our lives. He alone can enable us to live up to the pattern of life Jesus has set out. Jesus promises us that God will give His Holy Spirit to those who ask Him (Luke 11:13).

Only as we repent, put our faith in Jesus, and receive the Holy Spirit will we be able to put into practice the words of Jesus. In terms of the Sermon on the Mount this will be seen in who we are; our poverty of spirit, our mourning over our sins, our humility, our hunger and thirst for righteousness, our mercy, our purity of heart, our peacemaking, and our rejoicing when we are attacked because of our faith. It will be seen in how we live; as the salt of the earth and bright lights in a dark world. It will be seen in our righteous lives; not being angry with fellow believers, but rather being reconciled; in our ruthless control of lust, in our not even contemplating divorce, in living lives with complete integrity, in turning the other cheek when attacked, and loving our enemies.

It will be made evident by our secret life of giving to the needy, praying and fasting, and in our forgiveness of those who sin against us. It will show itself in the fact that we store up treasures in heaven and not on earth; that we make God's kingdom and His righteousness the supreme priority of our lives. It will be revealed in our relationships; that we are not judgmental about others; that we seek God with all our hearts and that we do to others what we would have them do to us. Finally, it will show itself in our commitment to enter through the narrow gate, and to build our lives upon the rock.

What is the authority behind all this? Its authority derives from the preacher. The people who heard Jesus were "amazed" (vs. 28). They were, to use the literal translation "dumbfounded." Jesus was not producing secondhand stuff. He was not like "their teachers of the law" (vs. 29) who taught derivatively. Unlike them He did not teach with an endless string of quotations from commentaries and famous names. He did not even teach like the Old Testament prophets who began, "Thus saith the Lord." Rather He declared, "I say unto you. . . ." He did not teach by authority, but taught as one who had authority (vs. 29). As John Stott points out, He claimed the authority of a teacher, the Christ, the Lord, Savior, Judge and criterion of judgment; Son of God, and indeed of God Himself. "He teaches with the authority of God and lays down the law of God."[136]

We have to decide whether we believe what Jesus is saying is true and whether we will act on it. The Sermon on the Mount is not simply "good moral teaching." Jesus presents us with a radical, life-transforming challenge—indeed, the ultimate challenge.

Notes

1. Michael Green, *Matthew for Today* (Hodder & Stoughton, 1988), p 69.
2. A. B. Bruce, *Commentary on the Synoptic Gospels* (Hodder & Stoughton, 1987), p 95.
3. D. Martyn Lloyd-Jones, *Studies in the Sermon on the Mount* (IVP, 1976), pp. 72-3.
4. William Barclay, *The Daily Study Bible, Matthew 1–10* (The Saint Andrew Press, 1975), p. 99.
5. Fiona Gibson, *Daily Mail*, 9.2.93.
6. William Shakespeare, *The Merchant of Venice* (Act IV, Scene I).
7. John Wimber with Kevin Springer, *Power Healing* (Hodder & Stoughton, 1986), p. 70.
8. H. G. Wells, *The History of Mr Polly* (Collins, 1910), p. 19.
9. See David Armstrong with Hilary Saunders, *A Road Too Wide* (Marshall, Morgan & Scott, 1985), pp. 92–7.
10. K. S. Latourette, *American Historical Review* (L I V, Jan 1949), p. 272.
11. John Stott, *Christian Counter-Culture* (IVP, 1978), p. 65.
12. John Stott, *Issues Facing Christians Today* (Marshall Pickering, 1984).
13. *Ibid*, see pp. 113–129.
14. K. S. Latourette, *History of the Expansion of Christianity* (Eyre and Spottiswoode, 1945), Vol. 7, pp. 503–4.
15. Reprinted by arrangement with the heirs to the Estate of Martin Luther King, Jr, c/o Joan Davies Agency as agent for the proprietor. Copyright 1968 by Martin Luther King, Jr.

16. Much of this material is gleaned from and is an attempt to precis Chris Wright's *Knowing Jesus through the Old Testament* (Marshall Pickering, 1992).

17. John Wenham, *Christ and the Bible* (The Tyndale Press, 1972), p. 37.

18. The Old Testament law can be divided more or less into three categories. First, there is the moral law. These injunctions are broad and generally applicable to all societies (e.g., the Ten Commandments). This law still applies to us today. Secondly, the Old Testament also includes what might loosely be described as the 'civil law': laws which are more specific and directed to the particular social problems of ancient Israel. Although the principles underlying these laws are valid and authoritative for the Christian, the particular applications found in the Old Testament may not be.

For example, Leviticus 19:9–10 says, 'When you reap the harvest of your land, do not reap to the very edges of your field or gather the gleanings of your harvest. . . . Leave them for the poor. . . .'

> It is misguided to try to apply this law directly to our society. It does not mean that efficient combine harvesters that gather up every stalk of grain are contrary to the will of God. The aim of this law is very clear, namely to allow the landless poor to collect some free food. Inefficient combines are of no benefit to the poor in our society, who usually live in city centres far from the harvest fields. But though this law is inapplicable literally in modern societies, the principles underlying it should still challenge Christian men to devise the most efficient means that can help the poor of our age. (G. J. Wenham, *The Book of Leviticus* [William B. Eerdman's Publishing Company, 1979], p. 36.)

As well as moral and civil law there is also ceremonial law in the Old Testament. The writer of Hebrews deals very thoroughly with the uncleanness regulations and the sacrificial rituals of the Old

Testament. The effect of his argument is that the practice of the ceremonial law is obsolete for the Christian. Nevertheless, as G. J. Wenham points out,

> It was in terms of these sacrifices that Jesus himself and the early Church understood his atoning death. Leviticus provided the theological models for their understanding. If we wish to walk in our Lord's steps and think his thoughts after him, we must attempt to understand the sacrificial system of Leviticus. It was established by the same God who sent his Son to die for us; and in rediscovering the principles of Old Testament worship written there, we may learn something of the way we should approach a holy God. (G. J. Wenham, *The Book of Leviticus* [William B. Eerdman's Publishing Company, 1979], p. 37.)

19. Dietrich Bonhoeffer, *The Cost of Discipleship* (SCM Press, 1959), p. 111.
20. Chris Wright, *op. cit.*
21. Gael Lindenfield, *Managing Anger* (Thorsons, HarperCollins, 1993), p. 80.
22. *The Times,* June 1992.
23. C. H. Spurgeon, *The Gospel of the Kingdom* (Pilgrim Publications, 1974), p. 27.
24. Stephen Gaukroger and Nick Mercer, *Frogs in Cream* (Scripture Union, 1990), p. 95.
25. Corrie ten Boom, *Guidepost Magazine* (Guildposts Assoc. Inc., 1972).
26. Alternative Service Book, 1980, p. 288.
27. *Ibid.*
28. Lewis Smedes, *Sex for Christians* (Triangle, 1993), p. 220.
29. Francis Devas, *Draper's Book of Quotations for the Christian World* (Tyndale House, 1992), 10235.
30. Lewis Smedes, *op. cit.*, p. 200.
31. *Leadership Today,* November 1987.
32. John Stott, *Christian Counter-Culture* (IVP, 1978), p. 89.

33. C. H. Spurgeon, *The Gospel of the Kingdom* (Pilgrim Publications, 1978), p. 28.

34. William Martin, *A Prophet with Honor* (Hutchinson, 1991), pp. 597–8.

35. Franklin P. Jones, *Quotable Quotations* (Victor Books, 1985), p. 393.

36. *Christian Leadership.*

37. *Leadership Today,* November 1987.

38. Andrew Cornes, *Divorce and Remarriage* (Hodder & Stoughton, 1993).

39. John Diamond, *The Times,* 21 May 1992.

40. Karl Barth, quoted in Lewis Smedes, *Sex for Christians* (Triangle, 1993), p.220.

41. Lewis Smedes, *op. cit.,* p. 216.

42. William A. Heth and Gordon J. Wenham, *Jesus and Divorce* (Hodder & Stoughton, 1984), p. 200.

43. Andrew Cornes, *op. cit.,* p. 484.

44. See Chapter 11. See also Christopher Compston, *Recovering from Divorce: A Practical Guide* (Hodder & Stoughton, 1993), pp. 40–45.

45. *Daily Mail,* June 1991.

46. See *Mishnah, Tractate Shebuoth* (M. Shebuoth IV:13), p. 7.

47. William Barclay, *The Daily Study Bible, Matthew* (The Saint Andrew Press, 1975), pp. 160-1.

48. C. H. Spurgeon, *The Gospel of the Kingdom* (Pilgrim Publication, 1974), p. 29.

49. Dietrich Bonhoeffer, *The Cost of Discipleship* (SCM Press, 1959), p. 125.

50. Martin Luther, 'The Sermon on the Mount', in *Vol 21 of Luther's Work* (Concordia, 1956), p. 110.

51. Mishnah Tractate Baba Kamma.

52. C. H. Spurgeon, *The Gospel of the Kingdom* (Pilgrim Publications, 1974), p. 30.

53. John Stott, *Christian Counter-Culture* (IVP, 1978), p. 107.

54. Corretta Scott King, *My Life with Martin Luther King, Jr.* (Hodder and Stoughton, 1970), pp. 365–9.

55. Alfred Plummer, *An Exegetical Commentary on the Gospel According to St Matthew* (Elliot Stock, 1910), p. 89.

56. Dietrich Bonhoeffer, *The Cost of Discipleship* (SCM Press, 1959), p. 130.

57. C. G. Montefiore, as quoted in William Barclay, *The Daily Study Bible, Matthew 1–10* (The Saint Andrew Press, 1975), p. 172.

58 The word for "hate" is sometimes used as a semitic idiom meaning "love less," e.g., Luke 14:26, "If anyone … does not hate his father and mother, his wife and children, his brothers and sisters—yes, even his own life—he cannot be my disciple," and also Matthew 10:37.

59. G. Vermes, *The Dead Sea Scrolls in English* (Penguin Books, 1987), p. 62.

60. R. T. France, *Matthew* (IVP, Eerdmans, 1985), p. 128.

61. Dietrich Bonhoeffer, *The Cost of Discipleship* (SCM Press, 1959), p. 134.

62. H. B. Dehqani, *The Hard Awakening* (SPCK, 1981), p. 113.

63. W. F. Arndt and F. W. Gingrich, *A Greek–English Lexicon of the New Testament* (University of Chicago Press, 1957), p. 651.

64. Dietrich Bonhoeffer, *op. cit.*, p. 137.

65. By kind permission of Christian Solidarity International. Mehdi Dibaj was later released and subsequently murdered.

66. Gordon MacDonald, *The Life God Blesses* (Nelson Word Ltd, 1994), pp. 29–33.

67. John Stott, *Christian Counter-Culture* (IVP, 1978), p. 126.

68. A. B. Bruce, *Commentary on the Synoptic Gospels* (Hodder, 1897), p. 116.

69. A. H. McNeile, *The Gospel According to St Matthew* (Macmillan, 1949), p. 73.

70. D. Martyn Lloyd-Jones, *Studies in the Sermon on the Mount*

(IVP, 1976), p. 333.

71. John Stott, *op. cit.*, p. 130.

72. C. S. Lewis, *The Weight of Glory* (Macmillan, 1949), p. 4.

73. Graham Twelftree, *Drive the Point Home* (Monarch, 1994), p. 81.

74. See Dr and Mrs Howard Taylor, *Biography of James Hudson Taylor* (Hodder & Stoughton, 1965), pp. 50–3.

75. Charles Dickens, *A Christmas Carol*, from *Christmas Books* (Oxford University Press, 1988), p. 6.

76. *Ibid*, p. 88.

77. John Wesley, *The Journal of the Reverend John Wesley* (The Epworth Press, 1938), p. 147.

78. Stuart Robinson, *Praying the Price* (Sovereign World Ltd, 1994), pp. 35–6.

79. Quoted in Richard Foster, *Celebration of Discipline* (Hodder & Stoughton, 1978), p. 41.

80. Stuart Robinson, *op. cit.*, p. 40.

81. Paul Yonggi Cho, *Prayer: Key to Revival* (Word, 1984), p. 103.

82. Andrew Murray, *With Christ in the School of Prayer* (Fleming H. Revell Co., 1953), p. 74.

83. A number of biblical texts state explicitly that God does not change (e.g., James 1:17–21; Malachi 3:6). However, there are also a number which appear to say that although God is unchanging in existence and righteousness, He does change in His decision and experience (Genesis 6:6f; 1 Samuel 15:11; 2 Samuel 24:16; Jonah 3:10). "The reference in each case is to a reversal of God's previous treatment of particular men, consequent upon their reaction to that treatment. But there is no suggestion that this reaction was not foreseen, or that it took God by surprise, and was not provided for in His eternal plan. No change in His eternal purpose is implied when He begins to deal with a man in a new way." (J. I. Packer, *Knowing God* [Hodder & Stoughton, 1973], p. 85.)

84. See Wayne Grudem, *Systematic Theology* (IVP, 1994), pp. 390–1.

85. Waymon Rogers, "Fasting," *Church Growth*, December 1988.

86. Mrs Howard Taylor, *Pastor Hsi Confucian Scholar and Christian* (Overseas Missionary Fellowship, 1900), p. 100.

87. Quoted in Arthur Wallis, *God's Chosen Fast* (Victory Press, 1968), p. 70.

88. Arthur Wallis, *op. cit.*, p. 25.

89. John Wesley, *Sermons on Several Occasions* (The Epworth Press, 1971), p. 301.

90. *The Independent*, 26.1.95.

91. John Stott, *Christian Counter-Culture* (IVP, 1978), p. 155.

92. Sheila Hocken, in a brochure for the British Council for the Prevention of Blindness.

93. Jackie Pullinger, *Renewal*, no. 161, October 1989.

94. William Shakespeare, *Othello* (Act III, Scene 3).

95. James Dobson, *Dr. Dobson Answers Your Questions* (Tyndale).

96. Dietrich Bonhoeffer, *The Cost of Discipleship* (SCM Press Ltd, 1959), p. 157.

97. Barry Humphries, *More Please* (Penguin Books, 1992), p. xiii.

98. N. T. Wright, *New Tasks for a Renewed Church* (Hodder & Stoughton, 1992), p. 131.

99. Title taken from a book by Dale Carnegie (Cedar, 1953).

100. Rob Parsons, *The Sixty Minute Father* (Hodder & Stoughton, 1995), pp. 36–37.

101. Cited in John Stott, *Christian Counter-Culture* (IVP, 1978), p. 166.

102. *The Times*, 9 January 1989.

103. William Barclay, *The Daily Study Bible, Matthew 1-10* (The Saint Andrew Press, 1975), p. 259.

104. Dale Carnegie, *How to Stop Worrying and Start Living* (Cedar, 1953), Chapter 1.

105. Fiona Castle, with Jan Greenough, *Give Us This Day* (Kingsway, 1993), p. 128.

106. *Evening Standard*, 11 March 1994.

107. *Alpha Magazine*, May 1995.

108. Graham Twelftree, *Drive the Point Home* (Monarch, 1994), p. 114.

109. Martyn Lloyd-Jones, *Studies in the Sermon on the Mount* (IVP, 1959–60), p. 484.

110. C. H. Spurgeon, *Lectures to My Students on the Art of Preaching* (Marshall Pickering, 1954), p. 123.

111. John Stott, *Christian Counter-Culture* (IVP, 1978), p. 178.

112. *Ibid*, p. 180.

113. Martyn Lloyd-Jones, *op. cit.*, p. 497.

114. Graham Twelftree, *Drive the Point Home* (Monarch, 1994), pp. 109–11. Lee Harvey Oswald was himself killed before his trial. Hence, it was never conclusively proved that he carried out the assassination.

115. Jonathan Sacks, *Faith in the Future* (Darton Longman & Todd, 1995), p. 18.

116. Joachim Jeremias, *The Prayers of Jesus* (SCM, 1967), pp. 96–7.

117. Obituary of Odette Hallowes, GC, *The Times*, 17.3.95.

118. William Barclay, *The Daily Study Bible, Matthew* (The Saint Andrew Press, 1956), pp. 271–2.

119. Martyn Lloyd-Jones, *Studies in the Sermon on the Mount* (IVP, 1959–60), p. 513.

120. J. C. Ryle, *Expository Thoughts on the Gospels: Matthew* (William Hunt and Co., 1878), p. 66.

121. Jonathan Sacks, *op. cit.*, p. 50.

122. Michael Green, *Matthew for Today* (Hodder & Stoughton, 1988), p. 89.

123. Walter Bauer, *A Greek–English Lexicon of the New Testament* (The University of Chicago Press, 1957).

124. *Hello!* no. 3224, 1 October 1994 (*Hola*, S.A., Spain).

125. James Dobson, *Preparing for Adolescence* (Regal Books, 1978), pp. 45–47.

126. *The Times*, 29 September 1994. By kind permission of Bernard Levin.

127. *Newsweek*, 17 October 1994.

128. It is clear that Matthew by no means polemicizes against prophetic proclamation, exorcism and acts of power, even though according to 7:22 the false prophets appeal to these. On the contrary. The fact that their emergence is so emphatically described as a sneaking in, as wolves in sheep's clothing, shows how like the other sheep their actions are. There must therefore be proper prophets who behave in similar ways, the difference being of course that these proclaim and perform love for one's neighbor which is no longer taught and practiced by the false prophets. . . . Not only healings of sick persons and exorcism, but even raising the dead are expressly promised to his disciples at 10:8, as they are reported of Jesus at 9:18–26. All these charismatic deeds should continue in the community as "deeds of Christ" and serve to answer all questions of doubt. (Edward Schweizer, *The Interpretation of Matthew*, edited by Graham Stanton [Fortress Press/SPCK, 1983], pp. 130–1.)

129. John Stott, *Christian Counter-Culture* (InterVarsity Press, 1978), p. 200.

130. *The Big Issue*, no. 29.

131. C. S. Lewis, from the Introduction to J. B. Phillips, *Letters to Young Churches* (Fontana Books, 1947), p. 9.

132. G. B. Caird, *St Luke* (Penguin, 1963), p. 107.

133. John Calvin, *Commentary on a Harmony of the Evangelists, Matthew, Mark and Luke*, I. (1558), p. 370.

134. Michael Green, *Matthew for Today* (Hodder & Stoughton, 1988), p. 92.

135. *Ibid.*

136. John Stott, *Christian Counter-Culture* (IVP, 1978), p. 222.

Study Guide

BY DAVID STONE

The Rev. Dr. David Stone has devised the following questions to help you get to the heart of what Nicky Gumbel has written and challenge you to apply what you learn to your own life. The questions can be used by individuals or by small groups meeting together.

1. How to Live under God's Blessing (Matthew 5:1–6)

1. Make a list of the four or five aspects of life that matter most to you. How do you think Jesus would respond to your selection?
2. Why is "happy" an inadequate way of translating what Jesus means by "blessed"? What would be a better way of expressing this idea?
3. What does it mean to be "poor in spirit"? What prevents people from developing this quality? How about you?
4. Under what circumstances would it be right for a Christian to be unhappy? What specifically does Jesus focus on here?
5. What is meekness? How is it related to inheriting the earth?
6. What does "righteousness" really mean? How desperate are you to be righteous? What tends to blunt your enthusiasm in this area?

2. How to Have an Influence on Society (Matthew 5:7–16)

1. "There is something very wrong with our society" (p. 22). What exactly do you think this is? Discuss ways in which you think Christians can make a significant difference.

2. What opportunities have you had recently to show mercy? How would you answer someone who said that showing mercy to others is a condition of receiving mercy from God?

3. What in practice would it mean for you to be more "pure in heart"? What benefit does this bring? How?

4. In what ways does Jesus call us to make peace? What situations can you think of where you could contribute something positive in this area?

5. Why will those who make peace be called "sons of God"?

6. What experience have you had of the opposition Jesus describes in verses 10–12? What is it that provokes such a reaction?

7. Why is persecution to be regarded as a blessing?

8. What truths about His followers does Jesus intend to convey with the illustrations of salt and light? How does this work out in practice for you?

9. What would you like people to say about you at your funeral? In what ways do you need to change so that they will?

3. How to Understand the Old Testament (Matthew 5:17–20)

1. Why do many people feel that the Old Testament is all about the time "before God became a Christian"?

2. Do you tend to treat the New Testament as more important than the Old? Do you think this matters?

3. What three main ways to look at the Old Testament does Nicky identify? How does Jesus fulfill each of these aspects?

4. In what way is Jesus' fulfillment of Old Testament prophecies more than just doing what they predicted?

5. How does Jesus "reveal the full depth" of the meaning of Old Testament law?

6. Can you identify the three ways in which Jesus fulfilled Old Testament law? How do these apply to you?

4. How to Deal with Anger (Matthew 5:21–26)

1. Do you agree with Gael Lindenfield's assertion that, under certain circumstances, you have a right to be angry?
2. When did you last get really angry? Was it right or wrong? How do you know?
3. How would you answer someone who claimed that getting angry is always wrong?
4. In practical terms, how can we avoid nursing angry feelings and so prevent them from escalating?
5. Why are even the "lightest terms of abuse" (p. 50) so dangerous? Is this how you see them?
6. What positive teaching does Jesus give here about how to deal with anger? In what ways does this apply to situations in your life?
7. What factors does Nicky identify as being involved in dealing with anger?

5. How to Avoid Sexual Sin (Matthew 5:27–30)

1. Why do you think adultery appears to be on the increase in our society?
2. Why is there "a tendency to think of sex as something degrading" (quoted on p. 58)? What adjectives would you use to describe sex?
3. Why does Jesus view adultery as a matter of thoughts and desires as well as actions and deeds?
4. What is the difference between looking at someone lustfully and appreciating a person's beauty?
5. How should we put verses 29–30 into practice?
6. What kind of "extreme measures" (p. 64) do you think Nicky is referring to? Do you feel that they are appropriate?
7. What are the seven steps which Nicky outlines for people who fail in this area?

6. How to Avoid Divorce (Matthew 5:31–32; 19:3–12)

1. What do you think are some of the common reasons for divorce?
2. On the question of the nature of marriage, do you agree with John Diamond or with Augustine? Which do you think is closer to the perspective of Jesus? Why?
3. What are the four conclusions that Jesus draws from the creation ordinance for marriage? How do these apply to you?
4. Why is the idea of a prenuptial agreement, which sets out who would get what if the couple were to divorce, so "totally contrary to the Christian idea of marriage"?
5. What difficulties are there in taking the view that Jesus did not allow remarriage after divorce?
6. Do you think couples where one or both partners have been divorced should be allowed to remarry in church? Why or why not?
7. What practical steps can people take to avoid divorce? How might these apply to you?

7. How to Live and Act with Integrity (Matthew 5:33–37)

1. What experience have you had recently of dishonesty in others? How did it make you feel?
2. How were people in Jesus' day abusing the framework that existed for making oaths?
3. What basic misunderstanding about God lies behind what they were doing? In what ways does this line of thinking affect us today?
4. Why does Jesus abolish the whole system of oath-taking?
5. Does what He says here mean that we should never take oaths of any sort? Why?
6. In what ways have you experienced the cost of maintaining honesty and integrity?

8. How to Respond to Evil People (Matthew 5:38–42)

1. What does the way in which Nicky tackles this specific issue illustrate about how Christians should tackle difficult issues in general?

2. What does *lex talionis* mean? In what ways was it originally intended to be operated? How was it being abused in Jesus' day?

3. Jesus gives four illustrations of areas where His followers are not to seek revenge. Can you think of modern equivalents for each of these?

4. How would you answer someone who felt it right to take Jesus' instruction, "Do not resist an evil person" absolutely literally on every occasion?

5. May a soldier who is a Christian kill an enemy? What issues does this question raise?

6. Nicky refers to the tension between being both a private individual and a citizen of the state. Can you think of examples of this tension in life today–particularly from your own experience?

9. How to Love Your Enemies (Matthew 5:43–48)

1. How had the scribes misinterpreted the Old Testament command "Love your neighbor"?

2. Who do you regard as an enemy? What three ways does Nicky suggest for you to love them?

3. What experience have you had of the harmful effects of hate on those doing the hating?

4. What reasons does Jesus give for His extraordinary command that His followers should love their enemies?

5. How would you reply to someone who claimed that the standards Jesus sets are quite impossible?

10. How to Give (Matthew 6:1–4)

1. How do you feel about the parallel between your "secret life with God" and the weight bolted to a yacht's keel? Why is our secret life with God sometimes easy to neglect?
2. How would you respond to someone who suggested that Matthew 6:1 contradicts Matthew 5:16?
3. As you think about your own giving, consider how much of your "reward" you have already received.
4. How would you advise someone who wanted to become a "cheerful giver"?
5. Do you find the concept of reward distasteful and inappropriate in a Christian context? What is the answer to this?
6. What does the Bible identify as the rewards of giving? In what ways have you experienced any of these?

11. How to Pray (Matthew 6:5–15)

1. Are verses 5–6 suggesting that it's wrong to pray in public? What is Jesus really getting at? How does this apply to you?
2. What can you do to reduce the distractions that get in the way of your time alone with God?
3. What key differences are there between pagan and Christian prayer?
4. What is the difference between the repetition in prayer that Jesus denounces and the persistence in prayer He commends?
5. Is there any danger of you praying the Lord's Prayer mechanically? How should this prayer be used?
6. How could you apply the requests in the Lord's Prayer more to your own life?
7. Take time to talk about any answers to prayer that you have recently seen.

12. How to Fast (Matthew 6:16–18)

1. How do you react to the idea of fasting?
2. What five reasons does Nicky set out for fasting? What experience have you had of these different aspects?
3. In what ways could you be "imaginative in fasting"?
4. What are the three main objections to the practice of fasting? How may these be overcome?
5. What practical advice would you give to someone who wanted to begin fasting?

13. How to Handle Money (Matthew 6:19–24)

1. How much of a priority for you is the acquisition of money? Why?
2. In what ways has Jesus' teaching about not storing up treasures on earth been misinterpreted? What does it mean?
3. What is wrong with seeking security by making lots of money?
4. In practical terms, how can we "store up treasures in heaven"?
5. What does Nicky mean by saying that "our hearts will follow our treasure"? In what ways have you found this to be true?
6. What does it mean in practice to have our eyes fixed on Jesus?
7. In what ways is money like a pagan god?
8. Is money your servant or your master? How do you know?
9. How can the power of materialism be broken in our lives?

14. How to Stop Worrying and Start Living (Matthew 6:25–34)

1. What do you worry about? What do you find this leads to?
2. In what ways has Jesus' command "Do not worry" been misinterpreted? What is wrong with these suggestions?
3. In what ways does your lifestyle reflect the truth that "Life is far more important than material things" (p. 159)?

4. In light of what Jesus says here, why is worry to be regarded as a sin?

5. Are you in danger of living your life "as though it were a dress rehearsal for the real thing" (p. 162)? What is the answer to this?

6. What does it mean in practice for you to "seek first God's kingdom"?

15. How to Handle Criticism (Matthew 7:1–6)

1. In what ways have people misinterpreted Jesus' command not to judge? How can we be sure that these are indeed misunderstandings?

2. What is Jesus getting at? How does this apply to you?

3. What negative consequences of disobeying Jesus in this matter does Nicky draw out? Can you think of ways in which you have experienced these?

4. Which would you prefer to receive—justice or mercy? Which do you tend to use in your relationships with other people?

5. Why should criticism of ourselves come before criticism of others? Does it with you?

6. What "pearls" do you possess (vs. 6)? What do you understand Jesus to mean by the "pigs" you should avoid throwing them to?

7. What "petty squabbles" (p. 180) are you involved in that need to be abandoned?

16. How to Get Our Relationships Right (Matthew 7:7–12)

1. How do verses 7 and 8 relate to the commandment to love God with all our hearts, souls, and minds?

2. What three reasons does Jesus set out for having confidence in God?

3. Can you think of an example of a prayer that you are now glad God didn't answer?

4. What does Nicky suggest should be our primary aim in life? Is it yours?
5. What is distinctive about the way Jesus formulated the "golden rule"? What difference does this make?
6. How is it possible for us as fallen human beings to demonstrate the sort of love that Jesus demands?

17. How to Find Life (Matthew 7:13–14)

1. Given the choice between a broad road and a narrow road, which would tend to be more attractive? Why?
2. When it comes to lifestyle, why is the narrow road so much to be preferred to the broad road?
3. To what extent is your Christian life characterized by "reckless abandonment" (p. 195)? Why?
4. What experience have you had of being in a minority as a Christian? How did it feel?
5. Why does Jesus describe the gate that leads to life as "narrow" and "small"? What does this mean in practice?
6. Are you on the broad road or the narrow road? How do you know?

18. How to Discern False Prophets (Matthew 7:15–23)

1. How would you respond to the suggestion that "if someone talks about God and heals people, what they say must be right"?
2. When Jesus talks about recognizing true and false prophets by their "fruit," what does He mean?
3. How are we to weigh the words of those who claim to speak from God?
4. By what criteria do you assess the sermons and talks you hear? What does Nicky suggest as the most helpful pointer?
5. What does it mean in practice to be "personally and vitally related to Jesus" (p. 211)?

19. How to Build a Secure Future (Matthew 7:24–29)

1. What are the similarities and differences between the two builders in Jesus' story? How do these relate to real life?
2. How would you help someone who thinks that life as a Christian should be free of problems?
3. Why would it be wrong to infer from what Jesus says here that we earn our way into the kingdom of God by good works?
4. What does it mean to put the words of Jesus into practice? How might you start (or continue) to do so?
5. Why is it entirely inadequate to describe the Sermon on the Mount as "good moral teaching"?

Alpha Resources

This book is an *Alpha* resource. The *Alpha Course* is a practical introduction to the Christian faith developed by Holy Trinity Brompton Church in London, England. *Alpha Courses* are now being run worldwide.

Resources needed for setting up, promoting, and training for the *Alpha Course*

- The *Alpha Course* Introductory Video
- *Alpha* Conference Audio Tapes –OR–
- How to Run *Alpha* Video (Volumes 1 and 2)
- *Alpha* Leader's Training Tapes or Videos (set of 3 talks)
- The *Alpha Course* Leader's Guide (one for each small-group leader and helper)
- How to Run the *Alpha Course:* A Handbook for Directors, Leaders, and Helpers

Resources needed for running the *Alpha Course*

- The *Alpha Course* Tapes –OR–
- The *Alpha Course* Videos (5-video set including 15 talks)
- How to Run the *Alpha Course:* A Handbook for Directors, Leaders, and Helpers

- The *Alpha Course* Manual (one for each small-group participant and leader)
- The *Alpha Course* Leader's Guide (one for each small-group leader and helper)
- Registration Brochures (one for each potential participant; sold in packets of 50)
- *Why Jesus?* (recommended reading for each participant)
- *Questions of Life* (recommended reading for each leader and participant)
- *Searching Issues* (recommended reading for each leader and participant)

In North America, these resources are available from Alpha Resources.

In the USA, call or write:

Alpha U.S. National Office
74 Trinity Place
9th Floor
New York, New York 10006
1-888-WHY-ALPHA (1-888-949-2574)
Fax: 212-406-7521
e-mail: resources@alphausa.org
www.alphausa.org

In Canada, call or write:

Alpha Canada National Office
P.O. 153, 3456 Dunbar St.
Vancouver, BC V6S 2C2
Tel: 800-743-0899 Fax: 604-224-6124
e-mail: office@alphacanada.org
www.alphacanada.org

Alpha Books
BY NICKY GUMBEL

Why Jesus?
A booklet recommended for all participants at the start of the *Alpha Course*.

Why Christmas?
The Christmas version of *Why Jesus?*

Questions of Life
The *Alpha Course* in book form. In fifteen compelling chapters the author points the way to an authentic Christianity which is exciting and relevant to today's world.

Searching Issues
The seven issues most often raised by participants of the *Alpha Course:* suffering, other religions, sex before marriage, the New Age, homosexuality, science and Christianity, and the Trinity.

A Life Worth Living
What happens after *Alpha?* Based on the book of Philippians, this is an invaluable next step for those who have just completed the *Alpha Course,* and for anyone eager to put their faith on a firm biblical footing.

Challenging Lifestyle
An in-depth look at the Sermon on the Mount (Matthew 5–7). The author shows that Jesus' teaching flies in the face of modern lifestyle and presents us with a radical alternative.

Telling Others
This book includes the principles and practicalities of setting up and running an *Alpha Course.* It also includes personal accounts of lives changed while attending an *Alpha Course.*

Heart of Revival
Ten studies based on Isaiah 40-66, drawing out important truths for today. This course seeks to understand what revival might mean and how we can prepare to be part of it.

30 Days
Follow Nicky through 30 days of focused Bible reading and prayer to see how God's Word and His Spirit can change your life. Start a new habit that will give life and energy to every day!

Alpha™

To order, call 1-800-36-ALPHA

Or visit your local Christian Bookstore